CORNELL
THEN & NOW

CORNELL

THEN & NOW

Historic and Contemporary Views
of Cornell University

Text by RONALD E. OSTMAN

Photos by HARRY LITTELL

McBOOKS PRESS, INC.
ITHACA, NEW YORK

DEDICATION

To our parents, Alan and Caroline Littell, and
Bernice and Henry ("Henning") Ostman

Library of Congress Cataloging-in-Publication Data

Ostman, Ronald Elroy.
  Cornell then & now / Ronald Ostman and Harry Littell.
    p. cm.
  ISBN 1-59013-045-6
  1. Cornell University—History. 2. Cornell
University—History—Pictorial works. 3. Cornell
University—Buildings—Pictorial works. I. Littell, Harry. II. Title.
  LD1368.O88 2003
  378.747'71—dc21

                                      2002155902

Distributed to the trade by National Book Network, Inc.,
15200 NBN Way, Blue Ridge Summit, PA 17214
800-462-6420

Additional copies of this book may be ordered from any bookstore
or directly from McBooks Press, Inc., ID Booth Building,
520 North Meadow St., Ithaca, NY 14850. Please include $4.00 postage
and handling with mail orders. New York State residents must add sales
tax. All McBooks Press publications can also be ordered by calling
toll-free 1-888-BOOKS11 (1-888-266-5711).
Please call to request a free catalog.

Visit our web site at: www.mcbooks.com.

Printed in China

9 8 7 6 5 4 3 2 1

CONTENTS

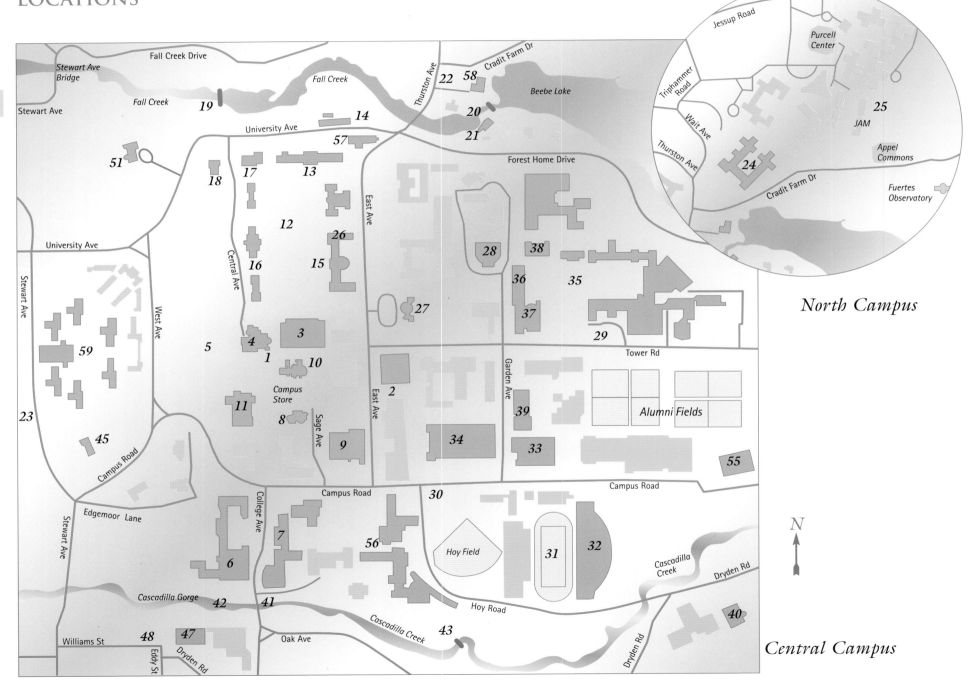

LOCATIONS

Fall Creek Drive

Stewart Ave Bridge

Stewart Ave

Fall Creek

Fall Creek

19

University Ave

14

57

Thurston Ave

22 58

Cradit Farm Dr

Beebe Lake

Forest Home Drive

20

21

51

17 13

18

Central Ave

12

East Ave

26

16

15

27

28 38

36 35

37

5

4 3

1

10

Campus Store

2

29

Tower Rd

Garden Ave

39

University Ave

West Ave

Stewart Ave

59

23

8

11

9

33

34

55

45

Alumni Fields

Campus Road

Campus Road

30

Edgemoor Lane

Stewart Ave

College Ave

7

6

56

Hoy Field

31 32

Cascadilla Creek

Dryden Rd

Cascadilla Gorge

42 41

Cascadilla Creek

43

Hoy Road

40

Dryden Rd

Williams St

48 47

Oak Ave

Eddy St

Dryden Rd

Jessup Road

Purcell Center

Triphammer Road

Wait Ave

Thurston Ave

25

JAM

24

Appel Commons

Cradit Farm Dr

Fuertes Observatory

North Campus

Central Campus

N

6

Map key and page locations:

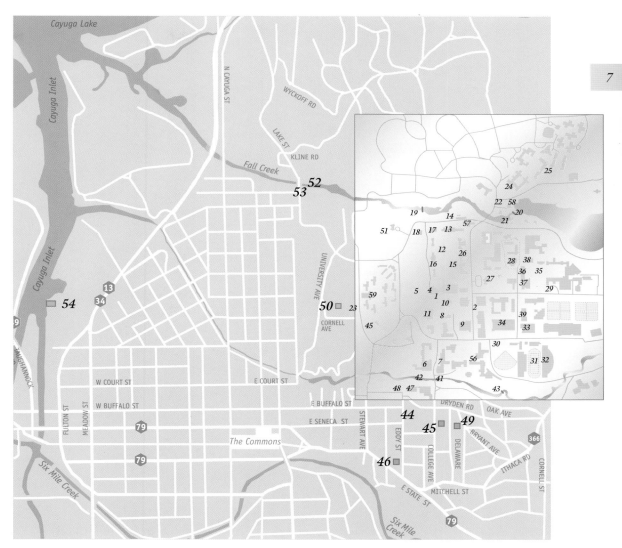

Collegetown and Ithaca

FOREWORD

8

"The art of progress," Alfred North Whitehead once declared, "is to preserve order amid change, and to preserve change amid order." The collection of photographs that make up *Cornell Then & Now* illustrates just such progress. Since its early days, there have been extraordinary changes on the Cornell campus, and they are strikingly demonstrated in these pages. But there is also order and, within the change, progress.

New campus areas are developed. The views of Sage Chapel and Cayuga Lake "then and now" are telling: what were once pastures give way to handsome new quadrangles. New buildings appear: Uris Library looms large in several views and the south campus buildings take shape. Progress involves not only change, but also creation.

Old buildings are demolished to make way for new. The South Barn is replaced by the Computing and Communications Center; Morse Hall comes down and the handsome Johnson Museum of Art, designed by I. M. Pei, goes up. Progress involves replacement.

Other older buildings, designed to serve one function, are restored, renovated, and converted to serve another: the Sibley School foundry becomes a sculpture studio, the A. D. White House a humanities center, the former Franklin Hall for electrical engineering becomes Tjaden Hall for fine art, and Sage College for Women becomes the home of the S. C. Johnson Graduate School of Management. Progress involves renovation.

Some photographs of the familiar are achingly beautiful, such as the A. D. White statue photographed by Margaret Bourke-White. Others are jarring: the tranquility of an earlier view of Libe Slope contrasts with the contemporary scene of Libe Slope on Slope Day.

Other things change little. In one view, Bailey Hall looks much as it did ninety years ago, though the seated president—a poised Andrew D. White—is replaced by a poised Hunter Rawlings III, and Miss Minns' Garden, now relocated, is replaced by Malott Hall. Progress involves continuity and order.

Still other scenes change not at all. The trolley-line bridge over Cascadilla Creek, the east side of the Arts Quad, and above all, the natural landscape are now much as they were a century or more ago. These things endure.

So the campus reflects the history of the University. Order amid change. Change amid order. And that is progress.

FRANK H. T. RHODES
Ithaca, New York
December 2002

ACKNOWLEDGMENTS

We acknowledge the many enthusiastic individuals who assisted in so many ways during the book's research and production phases. While it is not possible to recognize everyone in this brief space, we trust that all who helped will accept our thanks. Special appreciation is directed to the following individuals:

Those who helped find and make historical photos available, especially Elaine D. Engst, Director and University Archivist; Laura M. Linke and Nancy Lea Dean, Rare and Manuscripts Collection, Carl A. Kroch Library; John L. Ullberg, Landscape Architect of Planning, Design, and Construction; Gould P. Colman, former University Archivist, who also provided an invaluable fact-checking service; Kathryn ("Kasia") Maroney, Collections, and Andrew Weislogel, Prints, Drawings, and Photographs, Herbert F. Johnson Museum of Art; all of Cornell University. Thanks, too, to Mary Tomlan, Dewitt Historical Society of Tompkins County.

Those who helped with photographic advice, equipment, and copy work: Kent Loeffler, Morris Peck, William R. Staffeld, Jon Reis, and David St. George.

Those who helped with appointments and site arrangements, especially Anna K. Huntzinger, Executive Assistant to Cornell University President Hunter R. Rawlings III; M. Jay Wagner, Executive Staff Assistant to President Emeritus Frank H. T. Rhodes; Mike Brown, Boat Rigger (crew photo on the inlet); Paul A. Beckwith, Head Coach/Gymnastics, and Melanie Dilliplane, Assistant Gymnastics Coach (gymnasium area in Teagle Hall), and Ron Beck, owner, Louie's Lunch.

Those who made access to high places possible: Henry W. Crans, Director of Facilities, Arts and Sciences (Malott Hall, McGraw Hall Tower, White Hall); Mark R. Fabrizi, Building Coordinator, S. C. Johnson Graduate School of Management (Sage Hall); Curtis S. Ostrander, Deputy Director, Cornell University Police (Barton Hall); Michael W. Baughman, Building Coordinator, Athletics and Physical Education (Barton Hall interior); William ("Lanny") S. Joyce, Manager, Engineering Planning and Energy Management, and Thomas McCabe, Instrument and Controls Mechanic, Utilities Enterprises (Central Heating Plant smokestack); and the East Hill Flying Club.

Those who gave advice, information, and support, especially Mary F. Berens, Director of Alumni Affairs and Vice President of Alumni Affairs and Development; Richard E. Brown, Captain, Army Reserves and Assistant Professor, Military Science; Brian F. Chabot, Professor of Ecology and Evolutionary Biology; Candace E. Cornell, great-granddaughter of Ezra Cornell; David B. Collum, Professor, Chemistry and Chemical Biology; David C. Daniels, Sales Assistant, Cornell Store; Henrik N. Dullea, Vice President University Relations; Melanie M. Onufrieff, Head Coach/Women's Crew; Megan Perez, Reference Librarian, Olin Library; Linda VanBuskirk, Senior Lecturer, Ann Bianchi, Administrative Manager, and Joan Sweeney and Carol Adomiak, Administrative Assistants, Department of Communication.

Those who made cameo appearances in photographs, especially Cornell President Hunter R. Rawlings III and Cornell President Emeritus Frank H. T. Rhodes (others are named in photo captions in the text).

Research assistants (and stellar forwards on the women's ice hockey team!) Lindsay Murao '03 and Anita Khar '04.

To all the staff at McBooks Press, especially Alexander G. Skutt, President; Stephen Kimball, Production Director, Ellen Potter, Editorial Director; S. K. List, Editor; and Judy Dietz, Marketing Director.

And lastly, to our wives, Pat Fox and Nancy Ostman, for their encouragement and support.

"The start of all education, in the university sense, is a curiosity, and the end thereof is 'Let's go and find out'"

(Berry, 1950, p.104).

INTRODUCTION

In 2000, Harry Littell, author and photographer, brought out his revised and updated version of a wonderful book titled *Ithaca Then & Now* (McBooks Press), originally produced by Merrill Hesch and Richard Pieper. Harry is a graduate of Cornell University, and while his book did contain a few images of his alma mater, he naturally wondered what other historic photographs of Cornell existed. Harry knew of my interest in historic photographs and communicated his curiosity, wondering if we might collaborate on a new book if we found some interesting photos. We began our search in the Rare and Manuscripts Collections of the Carl A. Kroch Library, which also includes the University Archives. There were indeed some magnificent photos, and we have since learned that caches of photos exist elsewhere within the University and among Cornellophiles everywhere. We experienced major difficulties deciding which photos would have to be omitted. But we consoled ourselves by agreeing that this would be a "work in progress"

and that we would continue to dig through various collections in search of the *crème de la crème,* especially images touching on Cornell University topics that have not been fully reported or even broached. Because future editions are planned, we invite interested readers to contact us through McBooks Press to share relevant anecdotes, descriptions of photographs, corrections of fact or interpretation, and so on. We cannot be responsible for unsolicited materials, but we are very willing to make suitable arrangements to view one-of-a-kind images.

History depends upon primary and secondary sources. Historians always prefer primary materials (the "real thing"), but often must settle for someone else's review and assessment of the past. In constructing this book we have consulted both types of materials. We are very aware that different sources have given conflicting or contradictory facts and interpretations of those facts. We will be glad to rectify any grievous missteps we may have taken and to correct them in future

editions. Our goal is to provide a verisimilitude of truth, realizing that the absolute truth is impossible, even when one is a participant in an event of historic significance. Opinions and interpretations will vary from person to person. For the historian, complicating limitations are the selective deposit and survival of, and access to information. Kermit Carlyle Parsons, for example, describes how many of the official records of Charles Kendall Adams, Cornell's second president, were lost when they were cleaned out of university cellars for a wartime "scrap drive." Ditto for the College of Architecture's old records.

It is well known that photographs preserve information, often unintentionally. But it also is known that photographs can be constructed in particular ways to tell particular "truths." Therefore, we urge caution, both in viewing the photographs we've collected and in reading the accompanying narrative.

Our collaboration and project have been enormously stimulating, and we hope the book you now hold conveys

our sense of privilege in being able to undertake this adventure. We invite you to join us in shaping future editions.

RONALD E. OSTMAN
Ithaca, New York
June 2002

Thou seest an island, not to those unknown
Whose hills are brighten'd by the rising sun,
Nor those that placed beneath his utmost reign
Behold him sinking in the western main.
The rugged soil allows no level space
For flying chariots, or the rapid race;
Yet, not ungrateful to the peasant's pain,
Suffices fulness to the swelling grain:
The loaded trees their various fruits produce,
And clustering grapes afford a generous juice;
Woods crown our mountains, and in every grove
The bounding goats and frisking heifers rove:
Soft rains and kindly dews refresh the field,
And rising springs eternal verdure yield.
E'en to those shores is Ithaca renown'd,
Where Troy's majestic ruins strew the ground.

Alexander Pope, *Homer's Odyssey, Book XIII*

JENNIE McGRAW TOWER

A magnificent vantage point offering a breezy view, Jennie McGraw Tower is a venerable campus icon. Built in 1889 adjacent to Uris Library, the tower allows visitors to view and hear, at close range, the bells played daily. (Bring your earplugs!) While the view from the Johnson Museum is attained by elevator or stairs, the Jennie McGraw Tower view requires a climb of 161 steps—not for the faint of heart.

The ninth Cornell president, Frank H. T. Rhodes (1977–95), is pictured walking along Ho Plaza with Jennie McGraw Tower in the background. After stepping down from Cornell's top administrative position, President Rhodes has remained active on campus, and nationally. For example, he is author of *The Creation of the Future: The Role of the American University* (Cornell University Press, 2001) and *Successful Fund Raising for Higher Education: The Advancement of Learning* (Oryx Press, 1997). Rhodes was struck by an automobile in Florida in spring 2002, but has recovered from fractures and is walking again as he always has, with a brisk bounce in his step.

The Jennie McGraw Tower chimes are part of every Cornellian's misty memories. Jennie McGraw originally donated nine bells in 1868. They were the first chimes on any U.S. campus. Hung in a wooden tower on the site of Uris Library, they rang for the first time on the University's formal

opening, October 7, 1868. These nine bells display passages from Chant CVI of Alfred, Lord Tennyson's *In Memoriam*. The first exclaims: "Ring out the old, ring in the new; Ring out the false, ring in the true."

The tenth tenor and clock bell was donated in 1869 by President A.D. White, on behalf of his wife, Mary Amanda Outwater White. Its casting displays the Psalter version of the 92nd Psalm and verses by James Russell Lowell and it rings on the hour. The bells have migrated from the original ground-level playing stand on the site of the present tower, to McGraw Hall Tower (1873–91), to their present perch atop Jennie McGraw Tower, 173 feet high. Over the years additional bells have been donated, bringing the current total to 21. Other bells also have inscriptions, extolling, for example, "The Human Mind," "Knowledge," "Beauty," and "Virtue." A chimes museum in Jennie McGraw Tower tells the complete story.

Two selections from the chimes may be heard on the Cornell web site, www.cornell.edu. The "Jennie McGraw Rag," a 549-note piece that must be memorized by those who would become chimesmasters, is played at the beginning of each morning concert. The challenge is to play it as fast as possible, and more than one stopwatch has been put to the task of measurement and verification. The Cornell "Alma Mater," which closes each midday concert, also may be heard from the web site. Traditionally,

the "Cornell Evening Song" ends each evening concert. More than 2,000 selections—"the heartbeat of campus life"—are available to play in concerts, ranging from Schubert to The Beatles. After the expansion of the number of bells and their tuning in 1998–99, the chimes repertoire has continued to expand, thus adding to "that cheery tintinabulation that serenades Cornellians and visitors daily."

Another useful feature of Jennie McGraw Tower is the huge Seth Thomas clock, formerly installed in the tower of McGraw Hall during 1875. For many decades, the clock had to be manually wound, a two-hour job that would run the clock for a week. Today, the whole operation is automatic and programmable. According to chimes historian Ed McKeown, "Although they turn orange in October and green in March, McGraw Tower's four clock faces usually present a classic visage to the campus. The faces are made of white opal-flashed glass, and the hands are made of carved teakwood and painted black. Each face is ten feet in diameter. The hour marks are eighteen inches long, and the hands are about five feet long."

The Jennie McGraw Tower caught the attention of the world on October 8, 1997, when a spherical orange object, estimated to weigh sixty pounds—and later proven by a panel of scientific experts to be a *Cucurbita pepo* (pumpkin)—was observed to have been impaled at the top of the tower. This was no easy feat, because "the top 20 feet of the Tower is a steep cone and there's a lightning rod on top of it" (Mica, 1997). As the official University news release explained, "A giant pumpkin's mysterious appearance has been making national news (*New York Times,* Associated Press, CNN, MTV, NBC, etc.) . . . exactly how the pumpkin . . . was placed on top of McGraw Tower, and by whom, is still not known." Afraid it would fall (at an estimated speed of 72 miles an hour!), the University administration barricaded the area below the tower, replete with warning signs. Students got into the act, carving smaller pumpkins that appeared on the barricades. One carried a sign that read "Jump!" The tower pumpkin never fell.

Jennie McGraw Tower was undergoing routine masonry restoration at the time. A crane bucket was to hoist Provost Don Randal on Friday the thirteenth (March 1998) to the lightning rod spire to retrieve the "bright orange object" (as University administrators, tongue-in-cheek, still referred to it as of March 12). Workers making a practice run with the crane bucket, however, bumped the gourd that morning, perhaps due to a gust of wind, and it was knocked down, landing unharmed at the top of scaffolding 20 feet below. Provost Randal, joking that space aliens had put the bright orange object at the tower's pinnacle and now had decided to remove it, took the windy ride to the peak anyway, retrieving the object and bringing it to earth, to the cheers of hundreds of assembled onlookers. They had reason to applaud. While waiting for the provost, they'd enjoyed free pumpkin ice cream served up by Cornell dairy operations, and some also got a taste of a gingerbread model of Jennie McGraw Tower, topped, of course, with a candy pumpkin on its peak. The crowd, many clad in pumpkin T-shirts, clapped and shouted encouragement when a campus emergency vehicle whisked the object and Dr. John Kingsbury, Cornell Professor Emeritus of Plant Biology, away to the plant science building. There, the "Kingsbury Commission," headed by the good professor emeritus and four trusted additional Cornell experts representing plant breeding, vegetable crops, and fruit and vegetable science, did a necropsy, examining microscopic slides, poring over other physical evidence, picking through the gross morphology, and viewing video replays and photographs. Their unanimous conclusion, expressed in probably the shortest scientific treatise executive summary in Cornell history: "It is a pumpkin!" (Kingsbury, et al., 1998; *also see* Friedlander, 1998).

Herakles in Ithaka I, by Jason Seley

The pumpkin-placing perpetrators have never been discovered, nor have they come forward. One of the greatest campus pranks, so dangerous as to defy imagination—doubly so because it was accomplished under the cover of darkness at great height —survives in majestic myth. But, as shown at left, successive students have continued to play less intrepid pumpkin pranks during the Halloween season. Sculptor Jason Seley created his welded portrait, *Herakles in Ithaka I,* from 1980–81 and donated it to the Johnson Museum of Art. It stands between the Statler Hotel and Uris Hall. Herakles wore a new pumpkin hat November 1, 2001. The communication students shown in this image swore they knew nothing about it—(left to right) Yemi Rose (M.S. student) saw no evil, Emily Posner (Cornell Presidential Research Scholar in Communication '04) heard no evil, and Matthew Nesbit (Ph.D. student) spoke no evil. Whodunit? They didn't know.

Jason Seley was born in New Jersey in 1919 and graduated from Cornell in 1940 (art history). He returned to Cornell to teach, and chair the Department of Art, from 1968–73. He was dean of Architecture, Art, and Planning at Cornell from 1980 until his death in 1983. As described in an exhibition catalog, "[Jason Seley's sculpture is] . . . overtly constructed art, assertive, monumental, elaborative. . . . as welder/artist laureate, [he] gives with intelligence and technical mastery creative life to man-made materials previously shaped for other functions. Claiming as his medium the chromium-plated remains of automobiles, Jason has since 1959 transformed bumpers, hubcaps, bumper guards and exhaust pipes into an incredibly fluid outflow of forms . . ." (Bryant, 1977).

BOARDMAN HALL &
A. D. WHITE LIBRARY

The building in the foreground of this magnificent *circa* 1926–27 photo by Margaret Bourke-White is Boardman Hall, designed by preeminent Ithaca architect William Henry Miller, and the former home of the College of Law. Finished in 1892, the structure was named in honor of Judge Douglass Boardman, a trustee who had been a strong advocate for its construction and who served as the first dean of the law school. Boardman Hall was used by the Departments of History and Government after College of Law transferred to Myron Taylor Hall in 1932. In 1958–59, Boardman Hall was torn down to make room for Olin Library (opposite page), named for John Merrill Olin '13, an industrialist, trustee, philanthropic supporter of research (especially in veterinary science), inventor, and sportsman/conservationist.

Remnants of Boardman Hall are preserved outside and inside Olin Library. Outside, three Boardman Hall carved stone faces incorporated into a north-facing wall express worried resoluteness, angered readiness, and sleepy passivity. Inside Olin, another wall incorporates three more chiseled stone heads, overlooking the stairwell to the basement. Those countenances denote cocky bemusement, steadfast determination, and grim sourness. Legend says that likenesses of workmen who constructed Boardman Hall, Uris Library, and Stimson Hall were used as models for the busts.

Uris Library is glimpsed at the far right.

A.D. White was a bibliophile. His bequest to the University of some 30,000 valuable volumes became the foundation of the A. D. White Library (below), located within Uris Library. The White collection focuses on American and world history, with particular emphasis on the French Revolution, the American Civil War, architecture, Martin Luther and the Reformation, witchcraft, and miscellanea, including medieval documents and renaissance manuscripts, and works by John Milton and Galileo. The library is set in a three-storied space dominated by hefty books shelved within ornate galleried cast-iron stacks.

"The White Library is the only spot we know of in the whole world where one may be surrounded by the blues and golds of illuminated manuscripts, the loveliness of medieval art, yellow tomes, the concentrated wisdom of the ages, and at the same time gaze off forty miles at the raw scars the glacier cut here-abouts only yesterday—less than a million years ago" (Berry, 1950, p. 266).

URIS LIBRARY

Architect William Henry Miller's overall design for Uris Library echoes the cathedral plans of medieval builders, with a nave and transept within sight and hearing of a high altar—except that Uris Library's focal point is different:

". . . the architect here has grouped his system in four parts all radiating from the central delivery desk . . . taking advantage of the hillside . . . a third dimension is added, making the plan spherical. The book stacks, radiating from the delivery desk, are in seven stories, three of which are above and three are beneath the level of the desk. And the plan is such that the distance from the central desk to the extremity of the building, in any direction, up, down, or horizontal, is one hundred and twenty feet."

—*Guide to the Campus of Cornell University,* 1920

Why was the "central desk" a focal point? It was the center of book borrowing and loaning. Cornell was the first of the nation's universities to encourage undergraduates to check

out books and use them away from the library building. Today, Cornell's nineteen libraries house 6.8 million volumes, 7.6 million microforms, more than a quarter-million maps, 90,000 sound recordings, and 63,300 journal and serial subscriptions.

President White was eloquent in his praise for Uris Library during its dedication October 7, 1891: "This Library will be for generations, nay, for centuries, a source of inspiration to all who would bring the good thought of the past to bear in making the future better." Happily, his library also offers one of the most beautiful campus views of West Hill and Cayuga Lake. For booklovers, the setting is almost religious.

New York State granted Cornell University its charter in 1865. Ezra Cornell had made a fortune in the telegraph business and, with his eldest son Alonzo, donated 209 1/2 upland acres overlooking Cayuga Lake to serve as the academic campus. This gift and large financial contributions were made from August 10, 1866, to August 27, 1868.

Today Ithaca, New York, is proud of being "centrally isolated." Back when Cornell University was being founded, in the mid-1860s, Ithaca was isolated, period. Beautiful, yes, but isolated. Gould P. Colman, former University archivist, wrote of that period: "Much of the physical hardship of life at Cornell resulted from the efforts of getting there, for Ithaca was remote from any center of population and the University was hard to reach from Ithaca. From its wind-swept location the University was connected by a dirt road to the village then only beginning to extend up East Hill" (1963, pp. 44–45). Much has been made of the location and with good cause. The alma mater song, for example, notes the campus is located "far above Cayuga's waters" (actually 447 feet).

Romeyn Berry '04, '06, a popular campus columnist, described "A fantastic oddity, this [Cayuga] Lake which creates its own weather and possibly influences the tendency to independent thinking and doing which has always characterized the University that has grown up on the heights of its southern extremity! Foreign observers have more than once

divided American universities into three types: (1) the private, endowed institutions; (2) the great, State institutions; and (3) Cornell. More than once have we split tacks and drawn off from the others on a course of our own, and sometimes to the ultimate advantage of all" (Berry, 1950, p. 201).

The barn in the photo was on land well-trod by cattle. Ezra Cornell took particular pride in devel-

oping a model farm, which included a prize herd of American Shorthorn cattle for which he was renowned by 1858. The poles may carry either telegraph or telephone wires. This photo was probably made after 1878, since telephones were available in Ithaca by that year.

Cornell boasts one of North America's most beautiful campuses, due in no small part to the land-

scape's inspirational quality, with its attendant geology, fauna, and flora. The main campus sits on East Hill, above Ithaca on the plain below, with Cayuga Lake visible from some of the Arts Quadrangle buildings with northwest exposures, particularly those on the brow of "Libe" (for Library) Slope.

This particular contemporary view of Libe Slope is available but once a year. "Slope Day" is traditionally observed by students blowing off steam at the end of the last day of spring semester classes, before they settle into study for final examinations and write final term papers. Thousands gather to socialize, which, historically, for many also involves alcohol consumption.

Romeyn Berry admonishes, "Before you burnish up your own halo and indict the undergraduates of the present day for low crimes and misdemeanors, stop and ponder. When you were in college did you escape trouble because you were good and pure or because you were quick on your feet and had dumb luck?" (Berry, 1927, p. 62)

The University, trying to offset the alcohol focus of Slope Day, has offered a nonalcoholic alternative in "Slopefest," held in a closed outdoor area bounded by West Campus residence halls, with admission under supervised conditions. There, various activities and freebies are available, including live music, games, T-shirt tie dying, instant photographs with a life-sized cardboard stand-up of Cornell President Hunter R. Rawlings III, food and soft drinks, and games.

"Cornell University . . . students have never conformed to any recognized pattern. In appearance, thought, speech and manners they have always constituted a pretty representative cross section of the republic, with the human oddities slightly, perhaps, in the ascendancy. And I suspect that through the ages more ounces of pure gold have been recovered from the human oddities than from the mine-run of crude ore" (Berry, 1950, p. 252).

MYRON TAYLOR HALL

Between the wars, Myron C. Taylor '94, former president of U.S. Steel and later President Franklin D. Roosevelt's personal representative to the Vatican, donated a hall for the study of law. Of Gothic design and proportions, the building was well underway in this 1931 photograph. In the lower left, a workman stands, hand-chipping stone to be used as facing on the completed building. Myron Taylor also gave the University nearby Anabel Taylor Hall, likewise of Gothic design, in 1950–53, for Cornell United Religious Work (CURW), in memory of his wife. Today, Anabel Taylor also houses the Anne Carry Durland Memorial Alternatives Library and the Center for Religion, Ethics, and Social Policy (CRESP).

Myron Taylor Hall has been renovated and expanded (opposite page). Hughes Hall is attached, facing Cascadilla Creek and providing a residence for about eighty students. The Cornell Law Library has space for 443 scholars and features a world-class resource in online research, Internet services, e-mail, word processing, statistical analysis, and laptop connections.

Degrees offered include the J.D. (an average 3,200 applications for 180–185 seats); the LL.M. and J.S.D. (for foreign lawyers with American interests or other specializations—700 applications annually for 50–60 seats); J.D. with specialization in international legal studies; J.D./LL.M in interna-

Stone for Myron Taylor Hall came from the University quarry on Quarry Road, pictured at right in 1930. Workmen can be seen hand-working the stone in the quarry, surrounded by pastures, fields, and farms in the Turkey Hill Road region, south of Varna, New York.

tional and comparative law; and combined programs with the Johnson Graduate School of Management (J.D./M.B.A.), the Institute of Public Affairs (J.D./M.P.A.), the School of Industrial and Labor Relations (J.D./M.I.L.R.), the Department of City and Regional Planning (J.D./M.R.P.), and the Department of Philosophy (J.D./M.A. or Ph.D. in philosophy). The Cornell Law School also has joint programs with the Université de Paris I (Pantheon-Sorbonne) and Humboldt University in Berlin, which lead to a French law degree (Maitrise en Droit) and a Master of German and European Law and Legal Practice respectively.

Overall, some 560 J.D. students and nearly 60 international LL.M. candidates study at Cornell annually. Legal services to individuals unable to employ an attorney are offered by many law students as part of the Cornell Legal Aid Clinic. Students work closely with experienced attorneys in offering this service to those with legal issues related to women, religious liberties, the death penalty, and government benefits. Special programs also include instruction in legal ethics, legal information via the Internet, and a multi-year program in law and economics.

Today, the stone quarry is still operating as the Finger Lakes Stone Company, Inc., but has only a few years' worth of Llenroc stone left, which is being husbanded and saved for special Cornell building projects. Jim McKenna moves a boulder on a pallet with a forklift, at left.

24

The Armory (below) was designed by Charles Babcock and constructed at 4 Central Avenue in 1883. A gymnasium was added in 1892 as the north wing. The Armory's original purpose was to house the military department and hall. A large Armory field stood nearby, where Anabel Taylor (1953), Myron Taylor (1932), and Hughes Halls now stand.

In later years, the buildings and grounds were used for varsity team and recreational purposes (basketball, crew rowing practice, and roller skating), and as a medical clinic.

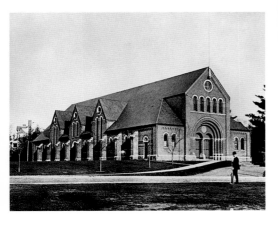

On special occasions, such as the Junior Prom, the Armory gymnasium doubled as a beautiful ballroom. Strings of lights and crepe paper, soft pillows and seats transformed the ordinary to a near magical venue. The *circa* 1910 photo at right was found in a physics professor's personal album. It shows the pride that students and faculty alike took in these socially important annual events.

In a diary entry, January 29, 1884, Charles William Curtis '88, civil engineering, wrote, "Went to a dance in the evening at Sage. Had a perfectly jolly time. We were permitted to dance till 11 o'clock—a most unusual event. Was tickled to watch Miss Nellie C— 'playing off and on' with some of the boys, but did not enjoy it so much where she tried it on me. I like her sister much better."

Also found in the papers (1884–1916) of Charles William Curtis, and

The Armory fell to the wrecking ball in 1956–57 to make way for Hollister Hall (below), honoring Solomon Cady Hollister, College of Engineering dean from 1937 to 1959. First occupied September 1, 1959, Hollister Hall houses the School of Civil and Environmental Engineering, which has eight specializations: engineering management, environmental engineering, environmental fluid mechanics and hydrology, environmental and water resources systems engineering, geotechical engineering, remote sensing, structural engineering, and transportation systems engineering.

his wife Stephanie Marx Curtis '88, bachelor of letters, was "At the Navy Reception," a newspaper article reviewing the Navy Ball at the Armory, on April 25, 1884: "The Armory presented its usual attractive appearance and the decorations for the most part were similar to those seen there at former balls. . . . At 9:30, the orchestra struck up, and the evening's enjoyment began, with no desire to hasten to a close. . . . The 54th Regiment Band of Rochester furnished most fascinating music. . . . But as the last number on the program was reached at about 3:30 A.M. all had become perceptibly weary and soon were willingly driven home in the carriages awaiting them, ere the echoes of music had been borne away upon the morning breeze."

The "Navy" was the Cornell rowing team which practiced and raced on Cayuga Inlet, or "The Rhine."

BARNES HALL & SAGE COLLEGE

Looking southeast from Jennie McGraw Tower during the late nineteenth century, one saw a pleasant vista, well landscaped around Barnes Hall (foreground) and Sage College (left), with fashionable professors' homes dotting East Avenue behind Sage College. Sage Avenue curved northeast from Central Avenue, then followed a north course beyond the west entrance of Sage College, eventually passing directly behind Barnes Hall. Sage Avenue continued northward beyond Sage Chapel (not pictured), where it curved west to join Central Avenue again at the location of Uris Library.

building beyond the spire of Sage Hall. It houses the Theory Center and the high-technology facilities of the College of Engineering. In partnership with IBM, Rhodes Hall's supercomputer is one of the world's largest and fastest, capable of 136 billion computations per second.

Also behind Sage Hall are the Statler Hotel and Statler Hall and Auditorium, constructed respectively in 1950 and 1958 (partial view, far left), to house the School of Hotel Administration. Ellsworth Milton Statler (1863–1928) was a hotel builder and keeper whose maxim is a foundation for the Cornell program: "Life is service. The one who progresses is the one who gives his fellow a little more, a little better, service." The school offered the first four-year educational program of its kind in the United States.

Campus growth has meant some crowding of buildings, as seen in the contemporary image. The campus store, however, was built underground (see white cover on the skylight, left foreground) to preserve the greenery around one of the oldest parts of the campus. Newer buildings include Olin Hall for chemical engineering (built in 1941–42) at right, sporting its row of twenty chemical exhaust vents. Buildings visible beyond Olin at mid-right are Bard Hall (1963–64) for materials science and engineering, Thurston Hall (1953) for theoretical and applied mechanics, and Kimball Hall (1950–53). Upson Hall (1958) for mechanical and aerospace engineering is at center, while Phillips Hall (1954–58) for electrical and computer engineering, Knight Laboratory, Grumman Hall (1958), and Frank H. T. Rhodes Hall are at left, beyond Sage Hall. Rhodes Hall is the curved

BARNES HALL

Barnes Hall was built in 1887–89, after a generous gift from trustee and New York publisher Alfred S. Barnes gave a boost to student contributions. Barnes Hall was erected for use by the Cornell University Christian Association (organized in 1869). Elm-shaded Central Avenue in the 1890s has been rutted by horse-drawn carriage wheels. Boards serve as crosswalks. Barnes Hall was the first campus building completed under the administration of Cornell's second president, Charles Kendall Adams (1885–92).

The trees fell victim to Dutch elm disease. Central Avenue no longer has much vehicular traffic at this location. Better known today as Ho Plaza, it primarily hosts pedestrians and almost all motorized traffic is restricted. Students frequently chalk pavement messages of social and political import for pedestrians' attention. Except for the concrete entrance walls, the underground Campus Store is unobtrusive in the foreground of Barnes Hall. Barnes houses the Public Service Center, the Cornell Career Services, the Office of Minority Educational Affairs, and a third-floor music auditorium. Glimpsed at the far end of Central Avenue is Snee Hall, home of the Department of Earth and Atmospheric Sciences.

"I want you to keep this letter until you grow up to be a woman and want to go to a good school where you can have a good opportunity to learn, so you can show it to the President and Faculty of the University to let them know it is the wish of your Grand Pa that girls as well as boys should be educated at the Cornell University."

—Ezra Cornell

Ezra Cornell had long expressed the hope and desire that women might one day attend Cornell University. In his diary entry of September 28–30, 1866, he wrote (spelling, grammar, etc., as in original): "Knowledge and truth is the only hope of our Nation secured through youth by a practical education, our daughters as well as our sons must equally share Blessings thus bestowed by our Countrys fostering care." He voiced a similar theme in a moving and revealing letter to his four-year-old granddaughter Eunice in 1867:

"I shall be very glad when I get through the business here [as a legislator in Albany, New York] so I can go home and see you and your little brothers, and have you and them go with me up on the hill to see how the workmen get along with the building of the Cornell University. I want you to keep this letter until you grow up to be a woman and want to go to a good school where you can have a good opportunity to learn, so you can show it to the President and Faculty of the University to let them know

it is the wish of your Grand Pa that girls as well as boys should be educated at the Cornell University."

Andrew D. White noted in his *Autobiography* that Ezra Cornell was earnest "in behalf of the higher education of women, and of their fair treatment in various professions and occupations" (1905, p. 314).

The desire for gender equity in education was apparent from the very conceptualization of Cornell University. It fell to Henry Williams Sage to make sure that the idea got off to an auspicious start. Sage became a Cornell University trustee on June 30, 1870, and five years later succeeded Ezra Cornell as chair of the board of trustees. He died September 18, 1897. At his memorial service, speaker M. Carey Thomas, president of Bryn Mawr College, was introduced by Cornell President Jacob Gould Schurman as "filial witness to the value of the higher education of women which the foundation of the Sage College made possible at Cornell University." Carey Thomas entered Cornell in 1875 at age 18 and immediately qualified for junior class status, based on

previous education and intellectual attainment. She graduated Phi Beta Kappa in 1877. She was determined to prove that a woman could excel in higher education, just like any man. Coeducation, she later said, was a "fiery ordeal." As Bryn Mawr's president from 1894–1922, she was an inspiration to generations of women, leading an institution that was a magnet for women, and which provided rigorous intellectual challenge.

"[I am] a loyal and grateful alumna of this university. . . . When in 1872, Mr. Sage advocated those principles of right and justice [higher education for women], expediency and economy, that in each successive year since then have opened university after university at home and abroad to women, not only co-education but the whole higher education of women was still but an impassioned idea. The first attempts to educate women on any large scale were then beginning only and even such few practical results as had been obtained were obscured, as always in the first years of any great reform, by the vehemence of controversial opinion. . . . In this great movement Cornell has been among the foremost, thanks to the wisdom, the insight, the love of kindness, the love of justice of Mr. Sage" (Thomas, 1897, pp. 52, 59).

The first woman was admitted to Cornell in February, 1870. Charlotte Williams Conable, Cornell alumna and trustee, estimated that 800 women were studying in U.S. coeducational higher education institutions that offered bachelor's degrees that year (Conable, 1977). Two factors had delayed women's admission, despite support from A. D. White and Ezra Cornell. First, the institution was immediately successful in attracting students. Conable reported that the entering class of 412 male students in the first class of 1868 was "the largest entering class of any American college of the period." Second, the social mores of the times demanded separate housing, which the University was not able to provide. Thus, the gift of Sage College provided a crucial facility, catering as it did to women alone. It

did not come in time for the first woman to attend Cornell in September 1870. She abandoned her studies due largely to the long and increasingly cold and bitter hikes up and down the hills every day from her distant lodgings. A. D. White thought this was particularly tragic, since the young woman had impeccable academic credentials. Not all faculty members (for example, Goldwin Smith) or male students agreed with the founders concerning the admission of women to study at Cornell, however.

"Mr. Sage some time ago offered to erect a handsome building for the use of female students . . . by this 'new departure' . . . opened our doors to students of both sexes, on the same equal footing. *Sic gloria transit*" (*The Cornellian*, 1871–72, p. 7).

"At the close of last year it was announced that, in future, ladies would be received into the University upon the same conditions as gentlemen. Some sixteen 'fair ones' have availed themselves of the proffered privilege, and we now find them in 'delicious juxtaposition,'

both in lecture and recitation rooms. The seraphic troop are manifestly exerting a 'softening' influence upon our underclassmen. Bravely facing storm and stare, they are quietly developing what will hereafter be of such use to them— we refer, of course, to their rosy cheeks—when they shall have been raised out of the darkness of ignorance, which has heretofore enveloped them, into that higher sphere, where are found the ballot-box, *crédit mobilier,* and manhood" (*The Cornellian*, 1873, pp. 7–8).

Eventually, however, the forces opposing admission of women to Cornell and the lack of a centrally located women's residence hall were overcome. Emma Sheffield Eastman, who transferred from Vassar to Cornell, became the first woman to be granted a Cornell degree in 1873. Two years later 29 women had taken up residence in Sage College, while another twenty women students used alternative housing arrangements. Of the fifty women studying at Cornell in 1884, half lived at Sage College (the college was able to house 120 students).

Anna B. Comstock, a legendary Cornell entomologist and a student resident of Sage College in the fall of 1875, remembered its accommodations and social life as "highly appreciated" and "inspiring" (Parsons, 1968, p.77).

When A. D. White was in his 80s, Cornell alumnae prepared a report summarizing the first twenty years of women at the University. Factual, literate, and convincing, that report concluded that "education in a great university did for women precisely what it did for men. It promoted intellectual growth, the full development of natural abilities, and often, the mastery of specialized skills." In short, two decades had demonstrated great success, thus justifying the early vision and optimistic confidence of White and Ezra Cornell in their advocacy for the University's inclusion of women.

SAGE COLLEGE & S. C. JOHNSON GRADUATE SCHOOL OF MANAGEMENT

Sage Hall, originally designed by Charles Babcock, has been brightened with a complete exterior refurbishing and is both functional and elegant with an all-new interior. The building has housed the S. C. Johnson Graduate School of Management since June 1998. The Johnson School is ranked among the nation's top ten business schools by *Business Week* and in the top five on a number of the magazine's important criteria. The doctoral program offers specializations in accounting, behavioral science, finance, management and organizations, marketing, production and operations management, and quantitative analysis for administration. This field of study began at Cornell in 1946 as the School of Business and Public Administration.

The atrium's dramatic 72-foot long skylight is a highlight of the new interior. The 5,100-square foot space has a 320-person capacity.

This view to the northeast, taken by G. F. Morgan from the roof of Sage College circa 1906, shows the stretch of land that spelled opportunity to University expansionists of the period. Two major and competing factions were interested.

The College of Agriculture saw the land as natural farming territory. The proximity of the New York State Veterinary College (which had awarded the nation's first degree in veterinary medicine) in James Law Hall and associated buildings east of East Avenue and south of the President's House (left, middle), as well as the newly built Stone, Roberts, and East Roberts Halls (left, horizon), home of the College of Agriculture, and the venerable Roberts Barn (left, horizon) gave this faction a strong claim to the land for experimental and demonstration purposes. Already the agriculturalists held claim to University farms, featuring greenhouses (white buildings, center) and barns (distant horizon, beyond the three-domed Fuertes Observatory).

The athletic and physical education group were also vying for land. Earlier athletic contests were essentially off campus, after their removal from the Arts Quad in 1890, with William H. Sage's gift of nine acres of land for athletic purposes at the foot of Fall Creek. The athletic field developed there, named Percy Field in honor of Cornellian Percy Hagerman, whose father financed a track, baseball diamond, stands, and buildings, was more than a mile away from Sibley College. This was inconvenient for students, faculty, and others in an era when transportation was limited and the vertical drop between campus and the field was some 400 feet. Besides, the Cornell Athletic Association, formed in 1889, already had a claim on the campus fields as a "play ground" and athletic field, comprising some 55 acres. To the right of these acres, however (not in photo), were more University farms and a small Garden House.

By 1910, the lines had been pretty well decided. Ultimately, Tower Road would divide the area into its separate fiefdoms.

The "faculty row" cottages seen in the foreground, as well as those homes just to the right of Fuertes Observatory on the near side of Garden Avenue (middle, right), were doomed, as their owners no doubt suspected by the time the photo was taken. An advantageous agreement with the University permitted faculty to build and live on the land very cheaply; however, the agreement also gave the University right of eminent domain. The land could be taken back if needed, upon reasonable compensation. Thus, the cottages (foreground, left to right) of Mrs. Robert H. Thurston (spouse of the former director of Sibley College), Professor W. L. Drew, Professor Willard W. Rowlee (botany), and Professor Henry Shaler Williams (geology) were destined for destruction.

The Fuertes Observatory fared better. The various manifestations of an observatory have traveled much since its original siting in 1888 on the west side of East Avenue. It was moved in the early 1890s to make room for the Dairy Building (now the north wing of Goldwin Smith Hall). It was moved again a few hundred feet south in 1901 to vacate the site for Stimson Hall. It next sat east of Sage Chapel and Charles Babcock's cottage, until it again was moved between 1903 and 1905. The incarnation seen in the photo above was funded by General Alfred C. Barnes of Brooklyn, member of the board of trustees. This was its fourth site until 1914. Today the site is occupied by Barton Hall.

At present, a different observatory lies north of Beebe Lake, built 1916–17. It is named for Professor Estevan Antonio Fuertes, former director of the College of Civil Engineering.

The contemporary photograph taken to the northeast from Sage Hall is much more claustrophobic in impression. The dark building ("Old Rusty") is Uris Hall (1972, named for Percy Uris and Harold D. Uris '25), housing the Departments of Economics, Psychology, and Sociology, and the programs of Cognitive Studies and Feminist, Gender, and Sexuality Studies, as well as an auditorium, Cornell Abroad, the Center for International Studies, the Center for the Study of American Political Economy, and labs for psychology, social psychology, and infant research. Immediately to the right of Uris are glimpses of Ives and Roberts Halls.

The large white building in the center is the Statler Hotel, a teaching hotel with 150 guest rooms, VIP and hospitality suites, and facilities used as part of the J. Willard Marriott Executive Education Center, which services 1,700 industry professionals from ninety countries annually. The School of Hotel Administration is a service-oriented management school with an international reputation for quality education, which uses the latest in computing, food laboratories, and beverage-management techniques. Annually, it educates about 850 undergraduates from the United States and 42 countries and offers master's and Ph.D. degrees to 120 graduate students. Sixty full-time faculty give the school, founded in 1922, a reputation as the hospitality industry's "think tank." In addition to traditional concerns with hotel and restaurant enterprises, the school also offers instruction relating to airlines, cruise lines, sports arenas, entertainment/amusement centers, senior living communities, automobile rentals, casinos, club management, real estate development, and many, many more facets of the burgeoning hospitality industry. To the right of the Statler is the peaked roof of Barton Hall.

SAGE CHAPEL

In the foreground of this *circa* 1888 photograph is Sage Chapel, Cornell's first nonacademic building. It was designed by the Reverend Charles Babcock (1829–1913), Protestant Episcopal Church rector and Cornell's first professor of architecture, whose personal house stands to the right in the foreground. Beyond the Babcock house is a "temporary" wooden laboratory and classroom building, hated by the architecturally sensitive president, A. D. White. It was the second building constructed on the quadrangle, built in 1868–69, and it stood until 1892. Immediately behind Sage Chapel stands the old stone row: Morrill, McGraw, White, and Franklin Halls. To the right of Franklin is Sibley Hall. The McGraw-Fiske mansion stands below the slope (center, left) with the magnificent view of Cayuga Lake in the distant haze. The tall mast between Sage Chapel and the mansion is a weather signal station. With a spyglass, Cayuga sailors could get the latest weather forecast through an ingenious system of signal globes.

Sage Chapel was built between 1872 and 1875 with funds supplied by Henry Williams Sage of Ithaca, who was chair of the board of trustees for 25 years after Ezra Cornell's death. Sage and President A. D. White placed two conditions on the gift: first, "the chapel would never be delivered over to one sect," and second, "students should be attracted but not coerced, into it" (Young and Stevenson, 1965, p. 14). Dean Sage, Henry's son, later endowed the position of chaplain, directing that divines of all denominations and faiths fill the post.

The contemporary view shows the many changes wrought to Sage Chapel and its surroundings. The white covered skylight of the underground Campus Store is in the foreground. Jennie McGraw Tower and Uris Library are behind and to the left of Sage Chapel. A portion of Morrill Hall's roof and the McGraw Hall Tower peek through, but the dominant structure in the center is Olin Library. Cornell's nineteen libraries house 6.8 million volumes, 7.6 million microforms, more than a quarter-million maps, 90,000 sound recordings, and 63,300 journal and serial subscriptions. To Olin Library's immediate right, a glimpse of the Sibley dome is visible. Buildings on the right side of the photo are Day Hall, Stimson Hall, and (barely visible) Goldwin Smith and Lincoln Halls.

The Memorial Antechapel, added in 1883 in the northwest corner of the chapel and funded in part by Jennie McGraw Fiske, was inaugurated by New York State Governor Stephen Grover Cleveland (U.S. President 1885–89 and 1893–97) who unveiled a tablet on the north wall on Commencement Day, June 21, 1883. Buried in the mausoleum are Ezra Cornell and his wife, Mary Ann Wood Cornell; their eldest son (and former New York State Governor) Alonzo C. Cornell and his wife, Elen Augusta Cornell. Also entombed there are the remains of President Andrew Dickson White and his first wife, Mary Amanda Outwater White, and two infant children born of the marriage between President White and his second wife, Helen Magill White. Also buried in the antechapel are John McGraw, his daughter Jennie McGraw Fiske, and her husband Willard Fiske (the first

University librarian from 1868–83), Edmund Ezra Day, the fifth Cornell president (1937–49), and his wife, Emily Emerson Day.

The original Sage Chapel Gothic-style structure, shown below, featured a 75-foot tower with spire and belfry. In January 1879, it housed one of the first two arc lamps in the United States, lighted by a dynamo constructed by physics professors William Arnold Anthony and George Sylvanus Moler, class of 1875.

Later alterations to Sage Chapel included the removal of the tower; the addition of an apse in 1898 at the east end to receive the bodies of Henry Williams Sage and his wife, Susan Linn Sage; a transept extension northward in 1903; and a west wing extension of the nave housing a baroque-style Aeolian-Skinner pipe organ in 1940–41.

Henry Williams Sage, called "the second founder of the University" donated the Chapel, Uris Library, Sage College for Women, the Sage School of Philosophy, and the Museum of Casts, during his lifetime.

Sensitivity to the role of religion at the University was due in part to early criticism of Cornell, made by individuals who objected to the institution's secular foundation, manifest in the fact that students were not required to attend religious services. Some went so far as to claim Cornell was "godless" and a corrupting influence on the students (White, 1905, p. 125), and that "indifferentism" would swell student ranks to "agnosticism and atheism" (Young and Stevenson, 1965, p. 149). Critics looked very hard for evidence. Professor Goldwin Smith's phrase, "Above all nations is humanity," (inscribed on a stone bench donated by Professor Smith, first placed outside Stimson Hall but which now stands outside the hall bearing his name) was interpreted by zealots as proof that nonsectarian Cornell University was irreligious.

"Because the College was not administered by some religious denomination and because the President had selected a corps of scientific lecturers and professors who valued truth more than legend, the churches were violently antagonistic. When the Press announced one fall that a large number—three hundred, I think—had entered the Freshman class, a leading denominational journal declared that 300 'fresh recruits for Satan' had entered this 'Godless college.' Another journal called it 'a school where hayseeds and greasy mechanics were taught to hoe potatoes, pitch manure and be dry nurses to steam engines.' We were even dubbed a 'Godless fresh-water college planted in Ezra Cornell's potato patch,' by the students of one of the older New England colleges. These and many other things of the same sort were hard to bear, for at that time we were not sure that we would laugh last" (Roberts, 1946, p. 136).

Many famous theologians, social activists, and distinguished persons have preached in Sage Chapel, among them Lyman Abbott, Martin Luther King, Reinhold Niebuhr, Paul Tillich, Daniel Berrigan, Elie Wiesel, and A. D. White Professor-at-Large John Cleese (also of *Monty Python's Flying Circus, Fawlty Towers,* and *A Fish Called Wanda* fame).

CRANE AND CALDWELL RESIDENCES & WILLARD STRAIGHT HALL

Professors had an option of building their homes on Cornell University land under an advantageous system known as "ground rent." They paid a $1 lease per annum to the University for land use and paid no taxes. The arrangement, however, also allowed for a $5,000 buy-out if the University reclaimed the land for academic expansion. The buy-out ceiling naturally limited the grandeur of the dwellings; perhaps for that reason, they were referred to as "cottages." A maximum of 42 ground rents were paid in 1910, with professors' cottages concentrated in the Grove Place, East Avenue, Reservoir Avenue, Circle, and Central Avenue areas. The University bought out all of these leases within the next several decades.

"Those attractive little homes of professors tucked in among the University buildings and scattered among the elm-shaded avenues have always been an interesting feature of the campus. . . . But now we become sadly aware that these campus cottages are doomed. Progress and expansion are ruthless things.

Sentiment cannot even check them. Nevertheless those who remember the old days cannot but be saddened by the passing of those pleasant homes. They kept the campus from being coldly institutional—merely park like. They gave to many generations of undergraduates little glimpses that cheered the homesick and the lonely. And the happy life that radiated from them had an effect on the entire tone of the University that cannot be supplied in any other way" (Berry, 1927, pp. 23–34, 26).

Moreover, the homes that fell to the wrecking ball also were valuable from an architectural point of view. Many were designed by William Henry Miller, in a variety of styles, ranging from Swiss to Italian Renaissance. For example, Professor T. F. ("Teefy") Crane's house at 9 Central Avenue, which was knocked down in 1924 to make way for Willard Straight Hall, was noted for its "interesting effect . . . reached by playing one heavy roof form against the other" (Dethlefson, 1957, p. 3).

Willard Straight's most historic moment is captured in this Pulitzer Prize–winning Steve Starr Associated Press photograph of the moment when African-American protesters vacated the building on April 20, 1969, after a forced occupation. Cornell was not alone in African-American student protests. According to William O'Neill, "Black militants dominated 59 per cent of the 232 campuses that experienced protests in the first six months of 1969" (O'Neill, 1971, p. 190). The Willard Straight incident, however, was the most publicized, due in no small part to Starr's photograph, which showed African-American **students** armed with rifles and ammunition belts. This was the first time that firearms had appeared as symbols in **campus** protests. The rifles were unloaded with breeches open as part of the negotiations to end the building's seizure, but the photograph did not readily communicate this:

"At 4:10 p.m. the front doors of Willard Straight opened and out came 120 black students, many of them brandishing guns. . . . A large group, estimated at 2,000, had gathered as word spread of the pending evacuation of the building. As the blacks emerged, a loud cheer went up, but they themselves remained silent as they marched across campus to their headquarters at 320 Wait Avenue. It was during this exit and march that the press and television representatives took the pictures which were seen around the world and gave such an ugly impression of the event" (*Campus Unrest,* 1969, p. 20).

continues . . .

Crane and Caldwell Residences & Willard Straight Hall

The Willard Straight protest . . .

Whereas confrontations on other campuses had led to extensive property damage and personal injury, the Willard Straight occupation resulted in "no bloodshed, no headlines of murder, no substantial property damage, no students hospitalized, and in very short order [the] campus was returned to relative peace" (ibid., p. 29). Despite the relatively calm resolution of the takeover crisis, the seventh Cornell president, James Alfred Perkins (1963–69) was criticized for his handling of the turmoil and left his post shortly thereafter.

Although Cornell University had fostered the founding of Alpha Phi Alpha in 1906—the first African-American fraternity in the United States—and many African-American students come to Ithaca to study, the racial tensions that led to the Straight's occupation continue to run deep. Today, "Open Doors, Open Hearts, and Open Minds" is the University statement on diversity, and an ideal that Cornell continues to pursue.

Shown in the historic 1923 John P. Troy photograph above, looking south from Jennie McGraw Tower, are houses once owned by (near to far): Professor George Chapman Caldwell, agricultural and analytical chemistry (demolished in 1924); Professor Thomas Frederick Crane, Romance languages and literatures (demolished in 1924); Professor James McMahon, mathematics; and Professor Ralph Charles Henry Catterall, modern European history. The fifth building was Sage Cottage, built by Professor Albert N. Prentiss in the late 1870s. It later served as a women's lodging house and as "University Club," a faculty accommodation. Distant build-

The construction of Willard Straight Hall, which opened in 1925, was, in part an attempt to make Cornell a more homey place for students. Willard D. Straight, a 1901 graduate of the College of Architecture, was an enormously successful diplomat, artist, journalist, diarist, musician, actor, dancer, interior decorator, entertainer, banker, financier, investor, publisher, soldier, Armistice negotiator, and supporter of the League of Nations. He died in Paris during the influenza epidemic of 1918 at the age of 38. His will requested that his wife "do something to make Cornell 'a more human place.'" The grand Gothic building that resulted, with its great hall, cathedral ceilings, marble staircases, oak paneling, and its many facilities and services—the Ivy and Okenshields dining rooms, ceramics and photography studios, exhibit spaces, browsing library and reading room, Cornell Cinema theater, art gallery, more than forty student organizations' offices, games, video, and music rooms, a bank branch, and a convenience store—continue to make it a magnet for student interaction.

ings include the homes of Professors Jeremiah Whipple Jenks, political economy and politics; Simon Henry Gage, histology and embryology; Edward Leamington Nichols, physics; Evander Bradley McGilvary, moral philosophy; and Irving Porter Church, applied mechanics and hydraulics. Also shown are Delta Upsilon and Delta Kappa Epsilon Lodges.

ARTS QUADRANGLE

In addition to his bequest of the President's House, A. D. White contributed generous financial assistance toward constructing the second campus building, known as "North Hall" or "North University," begun in 1868 on a site on the northwest corner of the present Arts Quadrangle. North Hall, an academic building, was occupied in late 1869. In 1883 the building was renamed White Hall in recognition of President White's many contributions. Given White's preference for grand gothic structures and "airy castles," this "honor" must have received, privately at least, a chilly reception. Over the years, White Hall has housed such academic specializations as architecture, mathematics, and medicine. A $12 million renovation of White Hall began in the summer of 2001 to accommodate the Departments of Government, Near Eastern Studies, and History of Art and the Visual Studies Program.

North Hall was half completed when the first building, begun in 1866, known as "South Hall," or "South University Building," and located at the southwest Arts Quadrangle corner, was opened in October 1868. South Hall was renamed Morrill Hall in 1883 to honor Vermont's U.S. Senator Justin S. Morrill, author of the Morrill Land-Grant Act of 1862, which enabled Cornell University to serve as both a statutory and a private, endowed institution. Ithaca historian Carol Kammen noted that Morrill's legislative initiative "provided the initial rationale—and means of funding—for the new institution. That act called for the teaching of agricultural and

engineering education, and for military tactics. These things were seen as important to the needs of the nation" (*Ithaca Journal*, 2001). Morrill Hall has served in various capacities over the decades, providing residential housing for students and lecture rooms, as well as space for administration; the alumni association (known as the "Cornell Council"); the Farmers' Wives' Reading Course, a predecessor of home economics; the College of Forestry; the College of Agriculture; the Departments of Anthropology, Modern Languages, Natural History, Psychology, and Sociology; the Laboratory of Experimental Psychology; the Hart Library of English Philology; the bookstore; a place to store general supplies; and a post office. Among the officials who were housed in Morrill Hall over the years are numbered the president, comptroller, treasurer, registrar, secretary, superintendent of buildings and grounds, and proctor. Of Morrill Hall's condition during the University's inauguration, Trousdale wrote that "the doors . . . stood wide open in welcome; in fact, they had to, as the hinges had not yet arrived" (1967, p. 202).

Morrill and White Halls are identified closely with the third permanent campus building, originally known as "Middle Hall." Like the other two names based on location, the name Middle Hall eventually was discarded and the building was renamed McGraw Hall for its benefactor, native Ithacan and original trustee John McGraw, who donated $120,000 to erect the facility, which housed a library, museum, and classrooms. Construction began with cornerstone-laying ceremonies conducted by the Grand Lodge of the Masons of the State of New York in June 1870 and was completed by October 1872.

The three original permanent buildings, constructed of local Cayuga bluestone, are aligned in "the old stone row" at the brow of Libe Slope. The early view on page 44, taken from West Sibley looking south, also reveals a building and a pole with signals at the top at the approximate location of the present-day Uris Library and Jennie McGraw Tower. This weather signal tower, whose mast is variously reported to be from 80 to 100 feet high, used large, colored signal globes to relay systematic meteorological forecasts, which were begun at the University in 1873. Also in view is the original mid-1870s configuration of Sage Chapel, which featured a tower with spire and belfry, since removed. The contemporary manifestation of Sage Chapel is larger as the result of additions at both the east and west ends in 1898 and 1940–41, respectively. Also of note is the gravel carriageway running parallel to the Morrill, McGraw, and White Halls, with an oval in front of McGraw Hall.

A 1920 campus guide noted of this trio, "This group of three halls is the nucleus about which the Campus has grown. In the [eighteen] seventies they lifted their unlovely mansard roofs above the bleak hilltop, where traces of pasture and cornfield were yet visible. Now the buildings of 'the old row' are adorned with ivy and shaded by tall elms; they are hallowed in the memories of Cornellians." Another perspective on the three buildings was offered, however, by Englishman Goldwin Smith: "Nothing can redeem them but dynamite" (Bishop, 1962, p. 91). The early campus architecture, historian Morris Bishop speculated, dramatized the temperamental differences between Ezra Cornell and

Andrew Dickson White. For Ezra Cornell, an austere Quaker, "grim, gray, sturdy, and economical" buildings would do. For President A. D. White, the aesthetic, contemplative intellectual, the "romantic upstate gothic, quaintly pinnacled and bedizened" structures of the President's House, Sage Chapel, Sage College, and Franklin Hall were more to his taste.

The present view of the same scene (page 45) evokes a similar mood in the hazy light of the early morning sun. The tree-bounded carriage drive has disappeared, replaced by footpaths crisscrossing the Arts Quad. Uris Library (built 1890–91, with additions in 1937) and Olin Library (constructed in 1960) may be glimpsed. Sage Chapel (built 1872–75) and Stimson Hall (constructed in 1901–03) are barely visible in the background. Students and faculty members of the mid-1870s would have no difficulty, however, orienting themselves in the contemporary scene.

"Cornell University, in common with many of the State Universities of America, had its origin in the Federal Government's grant, for the endowment of education, of a large portion of the public lands, under the authority of the Morrill Act, an Act of Congress approved by President Lincoln on July 2, 1862. Although it owes its foundation primarily to that grant, this University is indebted in a far greater degree to Ezra Cornell and Andrew Dickson White, to the one for its material wealth and to the other for its educational dimensions."

—Guide to the Campus of Cornell University, 1920

Hiram Sibley began his working life as a penniless shoemaker's apprentice. At age 21 he opened a machine shop, then graduated to banking and real estate in Rochester, New York, and eventually was said to be the wealthiest man in the city. His acquaintance with Ezra Cornell went back to Cornell's telegraph-business days. After Sibley got into the telegraph business in 1850, theirs was not a you-scratch-my-back-and-I'll-scratch-yours, "old boys" relationship. For years, they were on opposite sides of business dealings as principal antagonists. Eventually, however, in 1855, they joined forces in a company known as the Western Union Telegraph Company, for which Hiram Sibley served as president and Ezra Cornell was director and the largest shareholder. By that time, the once virtually bankrupt Ezra Cornell was rich and into the political and philanthropic phase of his life. He and Sibley became good friends, enough so that Sibley was named a charter trustee of the University, a post he held from 1865–88. Sibley did not have much to do with the very earliest

days of the University, however, evidenced by the fact that he never attended a board of trustees meeting until the 1870s.

President Andrew D. White was anxious for the University to fulfill the "mechanic arts" mandate of the land-grant legislation. This, he had to convince Ezra Cornell, did not include Cornell's idea of establishing great fac-

tories that would churn out chairs and shoes, thus providing employment and self-support for students. As President White diplomatically explained to Ezra Cornell, it was "exceedingly doubtful whether such a corporation could be combined with an educational institution without ruining both" (White, 1905, p. 371). White did not devalue practical experience. In addition to a

student's grasp of mathematics, thermodynamics, and drafting, he believed that Cornell graduates pursuing the mechanical arts "must have a direct, practical acquaintance with the construction and use of machinery before they could become leaders in great mechanical enterprises . . . [they must be] skilled workmen, practically trained in the best methods and processes" (White, 1905, p. 371). White struggled with various schemes concerning how this might be accomplished, at one point even investing his own money in the purchase of a lathe for students' use.

Enter Hiram Sibley and "a great piece of good fortune," as White put it. Hiram undertook the establishment of the Cornell unit that would blossom into an important part of the mechanical engineering program. In 1870, he pledged to erect and equip a college of mechanic arts. By June 1871, a building (now the west wing of Sibley Hall) was ready, containing the University print shop and shops for educational purposes. In the view on

the opposite page, it is shown years later with a horse and carriage on its south side, and Franklin Hall, now Tjaden Hall, to the west. To power the many pulleys and belts, water turbine power was carried from Fall Creek by wire cable to a dynamo room.

Eventually, Sibley College would be complete with lecture halls, drawing, drafting, and modeling rooms, a foundry, shops with forges for black-smithing, ironworking, and molding, and lathes and various tools for wood-working and carpentry. A map dated 1891–92, for example, shows "seven smaller structures north of Sibley and Franklin Halls . . . a rather untidy collection of inexpensive one-story structures that had been built to accommodate overflow from the very rapidly growing chemistry and physics departments and the College of Mechanical Engineering."

As Sibley College proved tremen-dously viable and popular, President White was delighted: "So began Sibley College, which is today, probably, all things considered, the most successful department of this kind in our own country, and perhaps in any country" (White, 1905, p. 373). This was not just the enflamed hyperbole of a proud president. *Scientific American* of October 17, 1885, devoted a cover article to Sibley College, featuring the college's Museum of Mechanism, in addition to all other elements contributing to its success.

After Sibley's death, his son Hiram W. Sibley continued contributing to Cornell in the spirit of his father's generosity. The father had constructed the west wing of what today is a continuous building (see page 47). The son was responsible for the east wing (built in 1893–94 as a separate building) and a dome that connected the west and east wings in 1901–02.

A foundry for the Sibley School of Mechanical Engineering was constructed in 1883 on the north side of University Avenue, near the Fall Creek gorge. The Foundry is the only surviving building of what once was a cluster of shops and industry-oriented buildings. Cornell, perhaps due to these early beginnings, awarded the nation's first doctoral degree in industrial engineering. Today, the Department of Art's sculpture studios occupy the space.

A. D. WHITE STATUE

This misty image was photographed by Cornellian Margaret Bourke-White '27, who was later renowned as a leading twentieth-century American photographer. At the time she took this photo, though, she was a typical student, trying to make enough money to stay in school. After arriving in Ithaca, Bourke-White lost out on waitress and library clerk jobs. Then, she recalled, "I chose Cornell, not for its excellent zoology courses but because I read there were waterfalls on campus. . . . it was the drama of the waterfalls that first gave me the idea. . . . Here I was in the midst of one of the most spectacular campus sites in America, with fine old ivy-covered architecture and Cayuga Lake on the horizon and those boiling columns of water thundering over the cliffs and down through the gorges. Surely there would be students who would buy photographs of scenes like these" (Bourke-White, 1963, p. 30). She had modest success selling her tiny campus photo views. Along the way, her architectural photos had attracted enough praise from Cornellians to allow her to dream of a career

as a photographer. Her diaphanous photographs were to give way to the more hard-edged, realistic, and documentary style for which she became famous.

Her subject for this foggy photo was the A. D. White statue, which is seated in front of Goldwin Smith Hall, facing Ezra Cornell's standing statue across the Arts Quad. White's likeness wears the gown of a doctor of civil law of the University of Oxford. The inscription at the base of the statue reads: "1832–1918. Friend and Counsellor of Ezra Cornell. And with him associated in the founding of the Cornell University. Its first president 1865–1885. And for fifty years a member of its governing board." The statue was one of the last major creations of Austrian-born sculptor Karl Bitter (1867–1915).

Sculptor Karl Bitter "was deeply impressed with the public career and extensive knowledge of President White . . . the kindhearted old gentleman who had seen to it that Ezra Cornell's university would provide a liberal education for the many and

later had worked for world peace at the Hague Conference . . . should be portrayed in a straightforward style that would not strive for polished perfection but would openly exploit the imperfect and the unfinished" (Dennis, 1967, p. 168).

EZRA CORNELL STATUE

Ezra Cornell's bronze statue was modeled by Hermon Atkins MacNeil (1866–1947). MacNeil was an instructor in the Sibley College of Mechanical Engineering and the Mechanic Arts before gaining national fame as a sculptor. The Ezra Cornell statue is located between Morrill and McGraw Halls. A simple inscription gives the years of Ezra Cornell's birth and death:

MDCCCVII–MDCCCLXXIV

(1807–1874).

Unveiled June 22, 1919, by Miss Mary Emily Cornell, sole survivor of the founder's sons and daughters, the statue honors the man who in the course of his life was a carpenter, farmer, factory and mill manager, practical engineer, implement inventor and improver, construction superintendent, businessman, member of the New York State Assembly and State Senate, and philanthropist. He was chair of the board of trustees from Cornell University's organization in 1865 until his death in Ithaca on December 9, 1874.

Seated on the platform are (clock-

wise): The Reverend Stephen Fisk Sherman; Miss Mary Emily Cornell, who unveiled the statue; third Cornell President Jacob Gould Schurman (1892–1920); Professor T. F. Crane; and Mr. Charles E. Cornell, grandson of the founder.

The sidewalk between the two statues of Cornell and White displays two sets of huge footprints, one set in white and the other in red. The foot-

prints lead from each statue to the center of the Arts Quadrangle where, campus myth says, the two men still meet to keep their friendship warm and to discuss the happenings of Cornell University. This occurs, the myth maintains, when a virgin walks across the Arts Quad at midnight.

Enjoying a summer concert at the base of the Cornell statue, these music lovers perhaps were not aware of Ezra Cornell's dream that "I would found an institution where any person can find instruction in any study." Cornell University's charter, under the Morrill Act of Congress, specified that instruction should be offered in agriculture and the mechanical arts (engineering), as well as military tactics. Cornell University was not prohibited from offering other scientific, humanistic, and classical studies, and both Ezra Cornell and Andrew D. White were eager to offer a curriculum that provided diversity and choice. Thus, music and the humanities were to stand on equal footing with any other subject matter and would certainly have a place on campus. The founders would no doubt be pleased to see the campus open to all to enjoy an outdoor concert. In their minds, this was an educational experience to be treasured.

"His evident desire was not to attempt the foolish impossibility of teaching every one every thing, but to recognize without reservation the equality of all search after knowledge" (Hart, 1913, p. 14).

"The figure of the Founder, frock-coated, stands with the right hand advanced and resting on a sturdy walking-stick. In this hand is held a wide-brimmed hat. The left hand, withdrawn, rests on a likeness of the Charter of Cornell University, which lies on a stand at the back of the figure. A leafy sprig of oak, symbolic of rugged strength, springs from the ground at the base of this stand. Behind the figure, on the stand is reproduced in the bronze the original Morse telegraph instrument."

—A Guide to the Campus of Cornell University, 1920

FRANKLIN HALL & TJADEN HALL

Between White and Sibley Halls, at the northwest corner of the Arts Quadrangle, is a building whose exterior celebrates chemists, physicists, and mathematicians—heroes of the departments that originally were housed in Franklin Hall. The building, designed by Charles Babcock, was completed as "fire resistive" in 1882–83. Since its construction, Franklin Hall also has housed the nation's first school of electrical engineering (which awarded the first EE doctorate), founded in 1889 and housed in Franklin Hall until 1954. Franklin Hall also has provided space for the art studios of the College of Architecture, as well as space for Asian Studies, the China program, and the Southeast Asia program.

Names and bas-relief images, mostly of eighteenth- and nineteenth-century science and math notables—nearly sixty all together—are found on every exterior wall of Franklin Hall. Some names and dates are covered with ivy. Others are worn into illegibility by time and the elements. Many, no doubt, are largely forgotten or unfamiliar to modern faculty and stu-dents. The names include, for example, Louis Berthollet (1748–1822), Humphry Davy (1778–1829), Joseph Priestley (1733–1804), and Justus von Liebig (1803–1873). The most prominent name, found at the main-door portico, is Benjamin Franklin's (1706–1790), commemorated with the inscription, "In honor of the First American Electrician. Erected 1881." Below, "Olive Tjaden Hall 1981," marks the building's name change.

Olive Tjaden Van Sickle '25 entered Cornell at age 15. In four years, she completed an architecture bachelor's degree that normally took five. From graduation through 1945, she and her associates designed some 400 mansions and homes in and around Garden City, Long Island, and another 1,600 churches, commercial buildings, and more in the New York City area. She was known as an archi-tectural pioneer and the leading

laboratory, a printmaking workshop, a studio for performance and installation art, and the Olive Tjaden Art Gallery. Instruction also is offered in drawing, painting, sculpture, and electronic imaging. The only historic interior accoutrement retained is a wooden staircase.

Great interest was generated when a new steeple, as near in appearance to the original as possible, was lifted to the southwest tower where the previous steeple, destroyed in a 1950s storm, had stood. The 20-ton, 30-foot replacement was lifted some 70 feet by crane. Wind gusts made the installation exciting for onlookers as two workmen in a steel cage, hoisted by a second crane, labored to position, bolt, and weld the new tower.

Roberto Bertoia, associate professor and chair of the art department, designed the tower's new peak ornament in the form of five arches, assisted by graduate art students Marc Parson and Will Pergl. The cast aluminum finial now joins the changing Cornell skyline, which has had two steeples restored in recent years (Sage Hall was the other recipient).

woman architect in the northeastern United States during that period. For many of those years, she was the only woman member of the American Institute of Architects and her work was on exhibit at the 1939 New York World's Fair. After 1945, she moved to Fort Lauderdale, Florida, where

she continued to design, mostly garden apartments. Olive Tjaden lived to be 92 years old and took an active interest in fine arts and the museum world, as well as architecture.

Tjaden Hall underwent a multi-million dollar restoration over an eighteen-month period, culminating in its

reopening in January 1998 as a brand-new building within the external shell of historic Franklin Hall. Housing the Department of Art of the College of Art, Architecture, and Planning, Tjaden boasts a six-story atrium, two student lounges, offices, multimedia technology classrooms, a photography

MORSE HALL &
HERBERT F. JOHNSON
MUSEUM OF ART

Today, the Herbert F. Johnson Museum of Art stands where Morse Hall, which housed chemistry, once stood. It was named for the inventor Samuel F. B. Morse, for whom Ezra Cornell laid the earliest telegraph wire from Baltimore to Washington, D.C., in 1843–44. Built in 1888, Morse Hall (right) was nearly destroyed by fire February 13, 1916. The top two stories were removed and the remaining two levels were roofed for the building's "temporary" use. It eventually was torn down in 1954. In addition to chemistry, which moved to Baker Laboratory in 1923, Morse held the College of Architecture's painting and sculpture divisions, the University's art gallery, and the theater division of the Department of Speech and Drama.

Cornell students in the late 1800s and early 1900s would not have found it strange to move from a sand-molding shop or a blacksmithing class to a drawing or art class. They enjoyed a lot of elective freedom and were able to combine classics and humanities, creativity, and practical hands-on skills in various subjects as part of the potent elixir Ezra Cornell and President Andrew D. White were brewing. Among all colleges and universities in the nation, Cornell had the distinction of endowing the first faculty chairs in American literature, musicology, and American history.

"All studies—the classics, the humanities, the sciences, pure and applied—become of equal dignity when pursued with enthusiasm and scholarly integrity. It was with that revolutionary postulate upon its lips that Cornell first crashed its way into the company of older foundations . . . with fantastic results . . ." (Berry, 1950, p. 189).

Those who wish to show off their campus to impress visitors quickly learn to ascend to the fifth floor of the renowned Herbert F. Johnson Museum of Art, designed by I. M. Pei. It occupies what President A. D. White considered the choice building site on campus. The Johnson Museum opened to the public in May 1973. The building won the American Institute of Architects Honor Award two years later. Little wonder. The fifth floor offers a spectacular 360-degree panoramic view, in addition to magnificent selections from the Johnson's Asian collection.

FALL CREEK
SUSPENSION BRIDGE

A study of Cornell maps reveals that a north-south suspension bridge was installed over Fall Creek between 1903 and 1905, at a point east of Morse Hall and the power station downstream. Today's suspension bridge has replaced the older bridge and is located farther downstream, immediately north of the Johnson Museum (barely visible, center horizon), which is on the site of the old Morse Hall. The footbridge gives pedestrians ready access to a large number of residences north of Fall Creek.

TRIPHAMMER FALLS & THE HYDRAULICS LAB

The early campus ended at the south edges of Fall Creek, Triphammer Falls, and Beebe Lake, which was created by Ezra Cornell's 1838 dam above the falls. Beebe Lake provided a dependable supply of water power for various grist, saw, woolen, gunpowder, and plaster mills below, as well as a foundry and furniture factories. Ezra Cornell himself managed a plaster mill for Colonel Jeremiah S. Beebe and answered at that time to the nickname "Plaster" Cornell. A wooden spiral staircase descended to the base of Triphammer Falls, trod only by daring, hearty souls.

Traffic to the site increased greatly after the "electric railway" crossed the newly erected Triphammer Bridge. Sibley College Physics and Experimental Mechanics Professor William Arnold Anthony, who taught at Cornell from 1872–87, was instrumental in starting the electric railway's streetcar/trolley line, only the second such system in the United States. It served the campus in the early 1890s, plying the passenger trade between the Delaware, Lackawanna & Western Railroad and the downtown Lehigh Valley Railroad railway station, from the Ithaca Hotel on the "flats," up East Hill with a stop at Cascadilla Hall, and across the University campus to Sibley College.

In 1897–98, Fall Creek gorge was spanned by a bridge that was more substantial than the existing pedestrian swing bridge, permitting vehicular traffic. The electric railway was extended across the new bridge in July 1899, finally giving the University easy access to the northern region beyond the gorge. A 1903 University map shows the electric railway route proceeding north across the bridge, turning west on Thurston Avenue, south to recross the Stewart Avenue bridge over Fall Creek gorge and continuing along Stewart Avenue, eventually looping back to State Street.

Today, three remaining footbridges cross Fall Creek: the Sackett footbridge at Beebe Lake's east end, the Triphammer footbridge above the falls at the west end of Beebe Lake, and the suspension bridge farther west below the Johnson Museum.

The Hydraulics Lab, extending about seventy feet vertically from the creek bed, was built against the southern cliff wall of Fall Creek gorge below Triphammer Falls (left) for the College of Engineering in 1902, at an expense of $7,390. The power house was built in 1905 at a cost of $10,000. Professor Estevan Antonio Fuertes, dean of the Department of Civil Engineering, first proposed the building to the trustees in 1896 as a laboratory for instruction and research in engineering and the testing of apparatus to measure the volume of water flow. Some reconstruction was carried out in 1961 and 1962, but eventually the Hydraulics Lab fell into disrepair. It now has broken windows and a crumbling southwest wall, which forms a gap where it formerly was merged with the steep sides of the gorge. In the spring, summer, and autumn, the abandoned Hydraulics Lab supports verdant plant life on its mossy, wet exterior. In the winter, it often is crusted and encased in ice and frost. Rusty pipes and faraway glimpses of shadowy stairways and floors, as well as its inaccessibility, exude an aura of mystery and perhaps stimulate an urge to explore for those who pause to peer into the gorge far below as they cross the Thurston Avenue bridge. Of course, not everyone has seen it quite that way. Robert H. Treman, Cornell graduate of 1878, said in 1930 that the Hydraulics Lab's "remains . . . have been an eye-sore for years" (*A Half-Century at Cornell*, p. 37). Hydraulics still are studied at Cornell in the DeFrees Hydraulics Laboratory, across from the Law School. Faculty and students study topics such as coastal engineering, wave hydrodynamics, and mixing/transport processes in the environment.

Just because there was a war on didn't mean a midshipman and his date didn't get hungry late at night. A favorite snack location then, as now, was "Louie's Lunch." According to David Hill, writing in the *Ithaca Journal,* this Cornell tradition first appeared on campus in 1918, toward the end of World War I. According to present owner Ron Beck, the business began with Louis Zerakes (also spelled Zounakos) and his pushcart. Louie began by catering to fraternities and sororities. *The Cornell Alumni News* of August 15, 1943, captioned this historic photo as follows: "Campus rendezvous. 'Louie' Zounakos does a thriving business these summer evenings in his 'dog wagon' at the usual stand on Thurston Ave. in front of Prudence Risley Hall." Visible in the dog wagon windows are grapefruit and graham crackers. A man and woman are inside, the woman wearing a hair net. A platform extends from the vehicle's running board to the sidewalk, where folding chairs await customers.

Various vehicles have served cold and hot meals to students, staff, and faculty ever since. Today, Beck and his staff cater to students out of a 1965 Ford, parked at the corner of Thurston and Wait Avenues from lunch time to 3 A.M. (evenings only on Saturdays and Sundays) while Cornell is in session. Favorites include the TBBC (a hot sub consisting of turkey breast, bacon, and cheese) and Louie's Chicken Parm. In summer, Louie's features lunches only. After the World Trade Center's destruction on September 11, 2001, Louie's Lunch joined the nation's wave of patriotism, its "God Bless America" banner echoing the omnipresent military uniforms seen on campus throughout the Second World War.

In the contemporary photo, Kent Loeffler, scientific photographer for the Department of Plant Pathology, and his wife, Kate Gould, a pastry chef, enjoy the cuisine.

On West Campus, gastronomes will find the "Hot Truck" operating from a 1983 Chevrolet, and serving nightly from its Stewart Avenue 600-block location. The Hot Truck began in 1960 as "Johnny's Pizza Truck," a mobile version of Johnny's Big Red Grill. Pizza didn't sell as well as hoped, hence the Hot Truck name. "Poor Man's Pizza" (toppings piled on French bread) and other menu specialties evolved. The Ithaca Shortstop Deli and Michael Smith currently run the business.

As David Hill wrote of these mobile snack bars, "Armed with grand-fathered-in special city permits and powered by specially built electrical outlets, they've become such a part of the campus experience that for many ex-Cornellians, homecoming isn't complete without a Louie's Chicken Parm or a Hot Truck Poor Man's Pizza" (Hill, 2001, p. 2A).

BALCH HALL

Balch Hall construction was begun in 1927 and completed in 1929 at a staggering pre-Depression era cost of more than $1.7 million. Despite the stock market crash of 1929, Cornell University moved ahead with the massive project to house women in the North Campus area, just north of the outlet of Beebe Lake, near Triphammer Falls. In the construction photo by J. Hubert Fenner, a tower of Prudence Risley Hall is seen, lower left. Risley, built in 1912–13, was a gift of suffragist Mrs. Russell Sage, named in honor of her husband's mother. It also housed women. The original dining hall is a copy of the Great Hall of Christ Church College, Oxford.

Much has changed, as shown by the contemporary photograph (opposite page) taken spring 2001. Visible are residence halls that followed Balch Hall: Clara Dickson Hall, built in 1945–48 (center, left); Mary Donlon Hall, 1961–62 (curved "Y" building); George Jameson Hall and Robert Purcell Community Center (towers, upper left); Townhouse Community, North Campus Residential Community, Ujamaa, Jerome H. Holland International Living Center, and Just About Music (smaller buildings clustered around Robert Purcell, tower at the top left); and the Hasbrouck Apartments (upper right). Helen Newman Hall, built 1963–65 (right, center), is used for physical education and recreation, such as bowling, fitness, and dance. Noyes Lodge, erected in 1958, and Alumni House, built in 1928 at 626 Thurston Avenue, are bottom right.

President Hunter Rawlings III made the development of North Campus one of the University's priorities, hoping to break down barriers and create positive cultural change by bringing all freshmen together in the same residential community for the first time in fall 2001. President Rawl-

together makes it clear to them that they're not alone [and] North Campus provides freshmen with leadership that meets these needs through the residence hall directors, student residence advisors, and programming that explores issues such as diversity, racial tolerance, sexual identity, or study skills."

The construction sites show the Court Residence Hall (center), the Mews Residence Hall (to the right of Court and Mary Donlon), and Appel Commons (above Helen Newman Hall, right) as workers rushed to complete the massive North Campus construction project, at an estimated cost of about $65 million, to house all 3,029 freshmen in the class of 2005.

Included in the 32-acre project are tennis and basketball recreational courts, a 625-seat dining facility, mailroom services, a cafe, a copy center, a school supply store, and a fitness center. Landscaping calls for 400 trees, which will make the area similar in appearance to the nearby Robert Trent Jones Golf Course.

ings announced this dramatic departure from Cornell tradition in October 1997. What was the rationale for bringing all freshmen together? It is intended to provide a common learning experience and environment for the freshman and to integrate intellectual and social life while enhancing

opportunities for interaction with faculty. Isaac Kramnick, the Richard J. Schwartz Professor of Government and Vice Provost for Undergraduate Education, put it this way: "When freshmen come to college, certain issues arise. They are suddenly away from their families, free from their

hometowns, and some of them feel lost, some feel lonely. For the first time they confront who they are. All of these developmental issues are not only part of transition to college but also part of the natural transition to maturity. Much of this comes to a head in the first year. Bringing the freshmen

DAIRY BUILDING & GOLDWIN SMITH HALL

Isaac Phillips Roberts, first College of Agriculture dean, noted that the original Dairy Building was constructed in 1892–93 after the New York state legislature had appropriated $50,000, "because Professor [Henry H.] Wing and I had taken such an active interest in the dairy husbandry of the State" (Roberts, 1946, p. 159). The building was made the north wing of Goldwin Smith Hall in 1905, when it became apparent that a larger, more modern dairy building was needed. Also, the agricultural campus was moving and expanding eastward, farther up the hill, where more abundant land, so necessary for farming, was available. The early picture shows the building wrapped in bunting in preparation for Spring Day, a major campus celebration in the same spirit as the contemporary campus spring favorite, Dragon Day. The first Spring Day was held on the Arts Quadrangle in 1902 and featured students in costumes, floats in a "pee-rade" (parade), and sideshows in tents for which admission was charged. The money collected, according to the May 18, 1905,

"Stunt Show" program, went to a good cause: "Being a humble effort on the part of Cornell undergraduates to have a good time and, incidentally, to extract from themselves and from their friends a few shekels to be employed for the support of their various athletic teams in their endeavor to bring added glory and renown to their beloved Alma Mater."

The 1904 poster advertising Spring Day read: "NO WORK!!! After 11 A.M. on Spring Day. The time will be devoted to viewing the Wondrous March Pee-rade de Luxe at 11 sharp::: The Indian Durbar, Scintillating Floats representing Historic scenes, the Poo Bah Indians (In War Paint), the Famous Dead Wood Coach Protected by Heavily Armed Cowboys and Pro-

minent Citizens in Carriages. Following which will come The Long Awaited Campus Circus, The Great Wild West Show, The Highly Moral Bench Show Exhibiting Mutts of all Nations, the Loop-the-Loop and a Thousand Variegated Midway Items, Decorative Fakirs, Hot Frankfurters and all the rest. And O! The main attraction at the Lyceum in the

dragon parades around campus before being burned on the Arts Quad. Engineering students traditionally act as antagonists. Many campus trees, especially those on the Arts Quad, receive a draping of biodegradable toilet paper for the occasion.

After its incorporation into contemporary Goldwin Smith Hall ("a Greek temple with bungalow trimmings" according to Morris Bishop), which opened in 1906, the Dairy Building, *a.k.a.* "the northern wing," is perhaps best remembered as providing the office for author Vladimir Nabokov (1899–1977) who taught at Cornell from 1948–59. Nabokov is best known for *Lolita*, his explosive 1955 novel. A plaque attesting to his Cornell residency hangs on the wall outside Room 278 today.

Many of the Spring Day and Dragon Day festivities took place in the Arts Quadrangle, which also served as a venue for early baseball and cricket games.

evening. Spring Day May 13" (Jacklin, 1974, p. iv).

In 1905, the Spring Day festivities attracted national attention and outrage. Shoddy journalism, widely printed in the newspapers of the day, claimed that Cornell students had sponsored a bull fight. While those concerned with animal cruelty were justifiably alarmed, what the students had actually done was to stage a simulated bull fight, complete with a papier-mâché bull on wheels charging a matador!

In the 1920s, Spring Day themes featured, "When Knighthood was in Flower," "Venice," and "Roman Circus." But it was during the 1901 Spring Day "pee-rade" that Willard D. Straight reportedly convinced his fellow student architects to dress as a dragon, eventually leading to the Dragon Day festivities, which replaced Spring Day. Robin C. Block '84 noted, "In the 60s Spring Day came to a halt. . . . Not only was there a lack of campus interest in serious fun, but also mischievous and dangerous pranks plagued the traditional day" (Block, 1983, p. 7). Dragon Day, which occurs around St. Patrick's Day, features an elaborate dragon built by freshmen architecture students. The

A. D. WHITE HOUSE

Andrew Dickson White was born in Homer, New York, on November 7, 1832. Later, the White family moved to nearby Syracuse. He studied at Yale and finished his A.B. in 1853, and later did advanced studies (LL.D.) in Paris and Berlin. He was 34 years old when he became Cornell University's first president. Already, he had taught history and English literature at the University of Michigan for six years. At Cornell A. D. White also served as professor of history and held the academic post of dean of the College of History and Political Science.

"Andrew White had discovered that to hear lectures on the history of America, he had to go to the Sorbonne; Cornell offered the first course in the country in American history, in a department graced by White and Goldwin Smith" (Guerlac, 1962, p. 8).

A widely-published scholar, White was best known for *A History of the Warfare of Science with Theology in Christendom* (New York: D. Appleton and Co., 1986), available in at least six languages during his lifetime. Guerlac

calls it "the first important book on the history of science published in the United States" (ibid, p. 8). President White said he found administrative duties "almost hateful," but was extremely effective nonetheless. He retired as president in 1885, after seeing the fledgling University through many harrowing events and issues during its first twenty years.

Drawing $50,000 from the family fortune, White planned and built the "President's House," begun July 29, 1871, through summer 1874. He moved his family to Ithaca the year the

1911, again designed by Miller. The entire structure was remodeled in 1921 for Cornell's fourth president, Livingston Farrand (1921–37), who lived there with his spouse until retirement. The garden east of the building, which extends to the Big Red Barn, is named for President Farrand. His successor and the fifth Cornell president (1937–49), Edmund Ezra Day and his spouse Emily Emerson Day lived in the house until 1951. In 1953, the house was altered again and became the Andrew D. White Museum of Art. Today it serves as the Andrew D. White Center for the Humanities. Several rooms also are used for special social functions. The Big Red Barn, built in 1874 to serve as President White's carriage house and stable, has also housed large animals associated with the College of Agriculture and College of Veterinary Medicine. It was first remodeled in 1955–56 and is used as the Graduate and Professional Student Center.

house was completed and lived there intermittently until his death on November 4, 1918. The architectural style of the house is High Victorian Gothic, one of White's favorites.

(Morris Bishop, writing in 1962, was less charitable, referring to the style as "Swiss Gothic.") It is located on a hill at 27 East Avenue. The structure was designed by William Henry Miller

(then a student in Cornell's class of 1868), who designed many Cornell and Ithaca area buildings.

The south library wing, shown in the contemporary view, was added in

Bailey Hall is named for Liberty Hyde Bailey, long-time dean of the College of Agriculture. As Guerlac wrote, "Liberty Hyde Bailey came to Cornell in 1888, and lent luster to the University and to the field of horticulture for seventy years. He is world-renowned for his monumental *Cyclopedia of Horticulture*. In 1935 he gave to Cornell the Bailey Hortorium of 135,000 mounted specimens of cultivated plants; and his research continued vigorously until his death at 97. Under Bailey's leadership the College of Agriculture became one of the great agricultural colleges in the world" (Guerlac, 1962, p. 11).

The small demonstration rural schoolhouse pictured in front of Bailey Hall was erected in 1913. It had two rooms, one a classroom and the other a workroom for practical instruction in domestic and agricultural subjects. A single teacher was able to monitor both rooms. That model of education passed out of existence, and the building later served as an editorial office for the *Cornell Countryman* and as a radio studio for originating agricultural and home economics programs.

Minns Garden, a memorial named for Lua A. Minns '14, once stretched along Garden Avenue in front of Bailey Hall. It consisted of demonstration plots tended by the Department of Floriculture.

The schoolhouse was demolished and Minns Garden relocated near the Plant Science building along Tower Avenue to construct Malott Hall in 1962–63, named for the sixth Cornell president, Deane Waldo Malott (1951–63). The building served the S. C. Johnson Graduate School of Management until the school moved to the renovated Sage Hall, and has served as the center for mathematics and statistical science since. Whether those changes were for better or worse may be debated by examining this early graduation scene, as the crowd spilled out of Bailey, compared with the view, opposite, of the parking lot now occupying the same area. The trees behind Bailey Hall in the historic photograph, along with houses formerly there, have made way for Savage Hall (1948), home of the Division of Nutritional Sciences, and Kinzelberg Hall (1997), which houses a variety of nutritional laboratories and the Office of Statistical Consulting.

A newer model of education continues to be associated with Bailey Hall. Its 2,000-person capacity auditorium hosts the nation's largest single lecture class, Psychology 101, "The Frontiers of Psychological Inquiry," taught each fall to 1,500 students by Professor James B. Maas, a member of the Graduate Field of Communication and a Stephen H. Weiss Presidential Fellow. He is also a frequent guest on national television programs as the primary author of *Power Sleep* (New York: HarperCollins, 1998), a *New York Times* best seller.

On the left in the contemporary photo are Clark Hall (built in 1965), which houses applied and engineering physics, the Department of Physics, the Lab of Atomic and Solid State Physics, the Cornell Center for Materials Research, the Physical Sciences Library, Science and Technology Studies, and the Hans Bethe Seminar Rooms. In the far left background is Olin Chemistry Research Laboratory, which, with Baker Laboratory, houses the Department of Chemistry and Chemical Biology. The Martha Van Rensselaer Complex on the right is home to the College of Human Ecology. The main building was built in 1933.

PRESIDENTS A. D. WHITE & HUNTER R. RAWLINGS III

"My soul is in this. The offer of my fortune and life for it is not the result of any sudden whim—it is the result of years of thought and yearning for better things in our beloved country."

There are now eleven Cornell presidents. The first was Andrew Dickson White, 1865–85, and the tenth, Hunter R. Rawlings III, served 1995–2003. These photographs show both men, separated by nearly ninety years, in front of Bailey Hall, built in 1912–13. President White, who lived to be nearly 86, was an eminent historian; President Rawlings, whose academic specialization is in classics, continues to participate in seminars in the social sciences and humanities and will step down from the presidency in 2003 to become a full-time teacher. Jeffrey S. Lehman was appointed Cornell's eleventh president by the Board of Trustees at a special meeting held on December 14, 2002.

As we look at this photograph of A. D. White toward the end of his long and productive life, it is well to remember that he had not achieved all that he accomplished by cold intellect alone. In an 1862 letter to the Honorable Gerrit Smith, A. D. White articulated his passion for establishing an institution of higher education, such as Cornell University was to become: "My soul is in this. The offer

of my fortune and life for it is not the result of any sudden whim—it is the result of years of thought and yearning for better things in our beloved country. No other bestowment seems to me to strike so deep or reach so far. None seems likely to be so long deferred if we cannot do something now."

President Rawlings, shown at age 56 in this photo, once faced a decision between a professional baseball career with the Baltimore Orioles and academia. A vigorous man of good humor, he accepted the photographer's props—Cornell alumni boater and cane—without murmur. He does not need a cane, nor could he, on this occasion, hold a somber face as the photographer requested!

SOUTHEAST CAMPUS

This undated aerial photo, looking to the southeastern portion of the campus, contains Day Hall (Administration) as its most recent building, occupied in 1947, but not the Schoellkopf west stands, built in 1948. Post-World War II Cornell was a different campus than it was before December 7, 1941, when the United States entered the war. Many veterans chose to continue their education via the "G.I. Bill of Rights," as the Serviceman's Readjustment Act of 1944 was nicknamed. The G.I. Bill provided great incentives to those who wanted to get ahead. By the time it ended July 25, 1956, it had provided $14.5 billion for education and training, with 2,200,000 of the 7,800,000 veterans who participated in the program having attended institutions of higher learning.

The lower part of the photo shows a number of long buildings that served as single men's temporary residential housing and as Baker Cafeteria. At the same time, many former soldiers, sailors, aviators, and other servicemen had started their families, so the University, with government assistance, provided adequate housing for a different kind of student—married with children. The mini-villages that were thus created were dubbed "Vetsburgs." One Vetsburg was located on East Tower Road, east from the Federal Nutrition Laboratory to Caldwell Road. Built in 1946, it contained 43 one-story houses with 136 apartments for family dwelling units. It was torn down in 1954 in preparation for new College of Vet-

erinary Medicine facilities. Still another Vetsburg was constructed in East Ithaca during 1946, just south of Maple Avenue, near today's Maplewood Park (in the upper right of the photograph). This 64-building complex came down in 1957.

Wartime navy facilities and immediate postwar Veteran Education and Administration buildings can be seen in the right center portion. The navy buildings didn't come down until 1954, while the Vet Quonset huts stood until 1962. Immediately across Campus Road from Sage Hall were buildings housing Industrial and Labor Relations. That area later became the home of various engineering buildings.

Most of the buildings in the historic photograph will be familiar to today's student, because they still stand. The older West Campus residence halls are located a third of the way up the photograph from the bottom (left to right: Boldt Tower, 1932; Boldt Hall, 1923; Baker Tower, 1916; North Baker Hall and South Baker Hall, 1916; Founders Hall, 1916; Mennen Hall, 1932; Lyon Hall, 1930; War Memorial, 1930; McFaddin Hall, 1930).

Up Libe Slope, in the row on the plateau immediately above the old stone row buildings on the brow of the hill (McGraw Hall, etc.) are, left to right: Goldwin Smith (1904–05), Boardman Hall, Stimson Hall, Day Hall, and Sage Hall. Above Goldwin Smith Hall is Rockefeller Hall (1904, roof visible). Above Rockefeller Hall are College of Agriculture buildings (to left of Alumni Fields, viewing

from bottom to top: Stone Hall, Roberts Hall, East Roberts Hall (all occupied in late fall, 1906), Plant Science (1931), and Rice Hall (1912). At the end of Alumni Field, top left, are Stocking Hall (1923) and Wing Hall (1913), with various barns and agricultural buildings behind.

On the site of present-day Ives Hall (occupied 1997), east of the corner of East Avenue and Tower Road on the south side of Tower Road, is James Law Hall and various associated buildings that formed the College of Veterinary Medicine, named for the Cornell Scottish educator who was the first person to give veterinary medicine instruction in the United States. Professor Law (or "horse doctor" as he frequently was called) came to Cornell for the inaugural year of instruction in 1868 and continued to 1896. Law Hall, built 1894–95, was torn down in 1959–60 to make way for Industrial and Labor Relations (ILR) buildings now referred to as the Ives Hall complex in memory of ILR's first dean, Irving M. Ives, who started the program in 1945. (Cornell offered the country's first four-year program in labor relations.) ILR also uses three additional buildings— the ILR Extension Building, the ILR Conference Center, and the ILR Research Building, all on the west side of Garden Avenue. Barton Hall and Schoellkopf Crescent are easy to spot toward the upper right. Just in front of the Crescent is the pyramidal Bacon Practice Cage. The twin smokestacks of Central Heating rise beyond the Crescent.

Southeast Campus

It is immediately evident that many buildings have gone up since the late 1940s. On West Campus, temporary residence buildings were replaced by the 1952–54 "U-Halls," or University Class Halls ('17, '18, '22, '26, and '28) and Sperry Hall, laid out in a cluster with Noyes Community Center at bottom right, just east of Stewart Avenue. University Avenue separates the University residence halls from the Greek houses (lower left). To the right of Willard Straight Hall stands the Gannett Health Center. To the right of Barnes Hall are Olin, Carpenter, and Hollister Halls. Behind Uris Library and Jennie McGraw Tower is the massive Olin Library, where Boardman Hall once stood (1892–1959). Along the east side of East Avenue, across from Day Hall and Sage Hall, are Uris Hall, the Statler Hotel, and Statler Hall and Auditorium. Behind the Statler are the many now-connected buildings that form the Ives Complex, home of the College of Industrial and Labor Relations. The engineering quad replaces the navy and veterans buildings. Hoy Field boasts a well-defined baseball diamond. Bacon Practice Cage is gone, replaced by a parking garage. Schoellkopf Press Box towers above the Schoellkopf west stands, now on the other side. A formerly densely wooded area at left center has become more sparse; the A. D. White House circle drive and the Malott Hall roof peek through. Beyond Rockefeller Hall stands the Space Sciences Building. At upper left, the Ag Quad has filled in, with tall Bradfield Hall dominating (upper left). At extreme upper left are Morrison Hall (1963), Boyce Thompson Institute, and a glimpse of the College of Veterinary Medicine. Riley-Robb Hall marks the extreme eastern boundary of the Robert J. Kane Sports Complex, while Wilson Synchrotron Laboratory lies to the south. The extreme western boundary of the Robison Alumni Fields is marked by Dale R. Corson–Seeley G. Mudd Halls and the Biotechnology Building. New Comstock Hall is just beyond the Ives Complex and Barton Hall. Teagle Hall is to its south. East of Teagle Hall, the curved western end of Lynah Skating Rink can be made out, with Bartels Hall connected farther east.

VIEW FROM THE CENTRAL HEATING PLANT

An early, limited version of central heating can be seen in the 1915-era Rice Hall photograph at right, which was taken to show an airplane ascending from Alumni Fields in the foreground. The large smoke-stack behind Rice not only certifies that the pilot was taking off properly into the wind, but that a major source of heat for the Ag Quad buildings existed.

John P. Troy, photographer of the 1922 pano-rama above, climbed up the Central Heating smoke-stack on September 13. His camera recorded a sweeping scene from Barton Hall on the extreme left, to the orchards on the extreme right. The trench across Alumni Field was dug for the installa-tion of steam pipes to the Ag campus.

continues page 82 . . .

PHOTOGRAPH
BY
J·P·TROY
SEPT-13-1922

CORNELL UNIVERSITY, 1902 AND 2001 PANORAMAS

Cornell University, 1902 and 2001 Panoramas Overleaf

The Seth L. Sheldon panorama, taken from the top of McGraw Hall Tower in 1902, does not quite cover 360 degrees. It looks northwest at the left and swings around to the southwest at the right edge. It will take a moment's study to figure out what the photographer and camera have done to warp the perspective in a way that the human eye never could. Of particular interest is the view of the final stages of the Sibley dome construction (left of center). An auditorium was housed under the dome in its early days; now, the dome is home to the Fine Arts Library. For many years it also housed the original Morse telegraph instrument that received the message, "What hath God wrought!" in Baltimore on May 24, 1844, using the line successfully laid, due to Ezra Cornell's inventiveness and guidance. Mr. O. E. Wood, Ezra Cornell's brother-in-law, was the first person trained by Samuel Morse to operate the instrument, and Wood had a hand in sending the message that day from Washington, D.C.

President Abraham Lincoln was remembered by Cornellians with the naming of Lincoln Hall, built in 1888. Lincoln Hall (right of center) is on the site of an old wooden laboratory building that housed physics, chemistry, geology, and the University photographer. It is situated on the eastern perimeter of the Arts Quad, between Goldwin Smith and Sibley Halls. During its history, Lincoln Hall served the College of Civil Engineering, as well as architecture, and contained the University museum. After remodeling and an addition, the building was rededicated November 2, 2000. It houses the Department of Music and the Music Library.

Harry Littell's 2001 panorama shows nearly 100 years of change. For example, the McGraw-Fiske mansion is replaced by Chi Psi. Morse Hall is replaced by the Johnson Museum. The Dairy Building is incorporated as the north wing of Goldwin Smith Hall. Boardman Hall disappears and Olin Library appears. And of course, when compared with the earlier view, most of the background magically has sprouted buildings, such as Baker Lab, Rockefeller Hall, Clark Hall, the North Campus, Bradfield Hall, Barton Hall, and so on. The only portion missing from this panorama is the West Campus residential area.

View from the Central Heating Plant
continued from page 78 . . .

The contemporary version of the view reveals that lands which haven't been given over to buildings have been permitted to grow up with trees. Dominant among buildings are the Biotechnology Building, Lynah Skating Rink, and Bartels Hall (left), Bradfield Hall (tallest, left center), the Wilson Synchrotron Laboratory (right, center), and buildings of the College of Veterinary Medicine (left of the smokestack). The F. R. Newman Arboretum of Cornell Plantations is on the horizon to the right of the smokestack. The water treatment plant and chilled water facilities are below and just beyond the smokestack.

Accompanying the photographer up the smokestack was Thomas McCabe, a Cornell instruments and controls mechanic.

SCHOELLKOPF FIELD & CRESCENT

Dominating the University sports complex are facilities honoring members of the Schoellkopf family. Schoellkopf Field and Stadium, home of football and (once) track athletics, were built in 1915 in memory of Jacob F. Schoellkopf of Niagara Falls, with seating for 9,000 spectators. That year Cornell was the national gridiron champion, placing two players, halfback Charles Barrett and end Murray Shelton, as All-Americans. Until 1924, when the Crescent was added, 119 automobile spaces were rented in two rows along the top of the stand east of the field for those who wished to view sports from the comfort of their cars. The Crescent took away the auto parking, but increased the seating to 20,950. The Schoellkopf west stands were added in 1948, adding 4,647 seats.

In the words of Romeyn Berry, "Football is not a game in the sense of being a diversion calculated to let the participant relax after the cares of the day and restore his mind and body with fresh air and exercise. It is a seasonal madness, to which few Americans are immune" (Berry, 1950, p. 142).

Schoellkopf Memorial Hall, built in 1915, bounding the north end of the field (left of center in Crescent photo) was given by Willard Straight '01 in memory of football player Henry ("Heinie") Schoellkopf '02, and contains the Robison Room Cornell Athletic Hall of Fame, as well as the George Brayman '22–Caesar A. Grasselli II '22 Condition-

ing Room, sports medicine, football staff offices, and football trophies.

Originally, a quarter-mile cinder track surrounded the football field. Today, the Robert J. Kane Sports Complex near Stocking, Wing, and Riley-Robb Halls and the Moakley Course (on the Robert Trent Jones Golf Course) are centers of cross country/

track and field outdoor activities. Barton Hall is used as the indoor track.

Also in 1915, the Bacon Practice Cage, which provided an area for indoor baseball practice during the winter, was erected (pyramidal building, center right above). Hoy Field, present-day home of Cornell baseball, is located west of the Schoellkopf

complex, just across Hoy Road from the engineering quad farther west (baseball stands partially visible, lower right of Crescent photo). Earlier baseball games were played at Percy Field, named for Percy Hagerman, class of 1890, located in the valley north of Fall Creek.

Hoy Field, today's baseball venue, is named for fabled David Fletcher Hoy, registrar and secretary of the Committee on Student Conduct, who began work at Cornell in 1894. Hoy was feared for his ferocity toward registrants. As registrar, Hoy had the responsibility of kicking failing students out of the University, a job he was reputed to enjoy sadis-

tically. However, he really had a "lamblike" soul, according to Berry, who saw tears in Mr. Hoy's eyes when he was told the new baseball field was named for him. Hoy always accompanied the baseball team on its spring trip south and took a particular interest in the team's fate. Hoy (never "Davy" to his face) is remembered in the Cornell song "Give My Regards to Davy." The lyrics are a burlesque on George M. Cohan's popular 1904 tune, "Give My Regards to Broadway." Other Cornell songs mentioning Mr. Hoy have the words, "Up in Morrill number three, Davy sits on my degree," continuing with Hoy's imagined advice to the faculty, "Bust 'em, bust 'em, that's the custom . . . " and "Cornell Universitee an' its bloomin' facultee Where old Davy raises thunder up in Morrill, No. 3 . . ."

The Paul A. Schoellkopf, Sr. '06 House (next to the Schoellkopf Memorial Hall), houses a lounge dedicated to 1971 first team All-American halfback Ed Marinaro. It, along with the Schoellkopf Press Box (tall building, right center), and Grumman Squash Courts (next to parking garage) complete the sports area south of Campus Road.

Recently, Cornell has fielded 36 intercollegiate men's and women's varsity sports teams, 18 for each sex. Some 1,100 varsity athletes compete annually.

SAGE COLLEGE & TEAGLE HALL GYMNASIUMS

Sage College was carefully and commodiously equipped and furnished. Special attention was paid to women's health and physical fitness, resulting in a gymnasium for their use. In this historic photo, taken in the Sage College women's gymnasium, the small banner on the wall to the right of the large Cornell banner commemorates Cornell University women's basketball. Legible winning dates include 1899, 1900, 1901, and 1902. The gym also contained a piano and two sets of tenpins, which hung on the right wall columns.

The 9,000-square-foot Teagle Hall gymnasium is used by the women's gymnastic team for training and competition. This state-of-the-art facility includes a Resi-pit system, vaulting runway, beam-and-vault area, spring tumbling run, and a full set of bars mounted over the pit. There also is a Tumbl Trak with a Resi-pit. Shown using the facility, which is considered one of the finest in the Ivy League and in the Northeast, is Allison Betof '05, biology major. She joins a team that has shown constant improvement and is setting school records for each event, including vault, uneven bars, floor score, and balance beam.

BARTON HALL

Cornell was cognizant of a new kind of warfare that came into increasing importance during World War I. The Wright brothers first flew a primitive airplane on December 17, 1903, in North Carolina. The airplane had developed to a sophisticated and important war machine by the time the United States fought in the Great War from May 1917 through November 1918. One type of American fighter plane manufactured during the conflict—the Thomas-Morse S-4C—was built by Ithaca industry toward the end of World War I. The "Tommy Scout" was a single-engine, one-seat bi-wing scout airplane, designed for pursuit pilots. In today's parlance, they were the fighter jets of 1917–18. From mid-1917 to December 1918, 497 Tommy Scouts departed Ithaca's Brindley Street and South Hill assembly lines. Brokered by the Ithaca Board of Trade, the Thomas-Morse Aircraft Corporation venture, begun in 1914, wedded the aeronautic expertise of William and Oliver Thomas and the financial backing of Morse Chain Company. At the height of production, thirty open-cockpit planes were

produced weekly. However, the Tommy Scout never saw combat.

Ithaca's participation in airplane production, plus cavernous Barton Hall and the campus military-mindedness combined to produce the scene opposite. Newly built and dubbed "Drill Hall," Barton was immediately put to use for officers' ground-school training by the Cornell School of Military Aeronautics, which occupied the premises from July 1917 through December 1918. The educational enterprise also featured barracks for 300–600 men, a temporary mess hall nearby, and laboratories to instruct them concerning engines, machine guns, airframes, and aerial observation techniques. Various airplanes are glimpsed in this 1918 photograph, under armed guard. Most of the airplanes obviously are not flight-worthy, because they are disassembled for demonstration purposes. Understanding of the strategic importance of wartime aviation clearly is evident, however.

Cornell produced four American aviation aces in the war, a status achieved by the confirmed downing of at least five enemy aircraft. The most famous was James Armand Meissner '18, who was in the first class to graduate from the Cornell School of Military Aeronautics on July 14, 1917. Meissner, the second American air ace, was a close friend of his squadron mate, Captain Edward ("Eddie") W. Rickenbacher, America's leading World War I ace, who wrote in his autobiography that Meissner had twice saved his life in combat. The

men served together for a time in the famous 94th Aero Squadron, which took the name and markings of "Hat in the Ring." Meissner later commanded the 147th Squadron and earned the Distinguished Service Cross and the Croix de Guerre. Another Cornell ace, Leslie Jacob Rummell '16, also took the same eight-week Cornell course as Meissner. Rummell became flight commander of the 93rd Pursuit Squadron and

scored seven enemy kills and the Distinguished Service Cross before his overseas death from pneumonia on February 2, 1919. The other two aces were Orrin Creech '20 and John O. W. Donaldson '21.

Alan Louis Eggers '19 was another highly decorated Cornellian. He was one of 41 American Congressional Medal of Honor awardees for conspicuous gallantry and intrepidity beyond the call of duty in action. He single-

handedly saved three companions under heavy fire. His other citations included the Distinguished Conduct Medal, the Medaille Militaire, the Croix de Guerre, the Croce al Merito di Guerra, the Portuguese War Cross, and the Montenegrin Bravery Medal. Eggers survived the war and returned to Cornell, completing a law degree in 1921.

Horses remained an important part of the military's means of locomotion and artillery transport during the first decades of the twentieth century. Equipment, horses, and student soldiers get their exercise in this John P. Troy photograph, with the early agricultural buildings on Tower Road in the background. Military artillery garages and riding stables, built in 1919, were located off Dryden Road, opposite the heating plant.

CORNELL CADET CORPS

As required in Cornell's charter, training in military science and tactics via the Cadet Corps and ROTC was part of the curriculum from 1868 onward. A course in military science was required of every able-bodied male citizen student during his freshman and sophomore years, with advanced courses available for credit as a junior or senior. Early class photographs depict some students wearing items from Civil War uniforms, both North and South. The 1870 *Cornellian* yearbook listed Joseph H. Whittlesey, Major U.S.A. Commandant, as professor of Military Science and Tactics. William E. Arnold, professor of mathematics, also was a major and taught military tactics. The military organization included the Commandant of Cadets, a brigade staff of three, a First and Second Battalion commander with three battalion staff members each (including D. S. Dickinson and E. L. Parker as principal musicians!), and four companies within each battalion, each composed of a captain, first lieutenant, first sergeant, and three sergeants. While not all companies were at full strength, it was an impres-sive fledgling organization, given 23 seniors, 62 juniors, 200 sophomores, and 286 freshmen on campus. Studies included infantry, field artillery, and signal corps tactics. Cornell was proud that the University's program ranked in the top ten to fifteen collegiate military training programs "of distinguished excellence" for many years, based on rankings by General Staff after annual inspections.

The military organization also served as a source of social entertain-ment. A military band was pho-tographed on parade in 1890. The "Military Hop" of the Cornell Battal-ion held at the Armory (also known as the Military Hall and Gymnasium, demolished in 1957) in the 1880s fea-tured a musical program consisting of twelve numbers, including waltzes, lanciers, polkas, and galops. Military training was mandatory for male stu-dents until 1960.

During World War I, Cornellians were quick to express patriotism, as seen in the John P. Troy photograph on page 92 of a "tent drill." Pup tents were pitched on the Arts Quad. Stacks of rifles were ready nearby. Inspections

and parades were a common order of the day. Simulated bayonet duels took place at Schoellkopf.

The war became real when a group of 35 men, under the command of Edward Tinkham '16, was on its way to serve as volunteer ambulance drivers in the service of France in 1917. When the United States declared war on Ger-many on April 6, they quickly volun-teered as ammunition drivers to the Aisne front on May 24. Thus, under the official designation of T. M. U. 526, they were the first American

East and West Hills echoed with the reports of cannon fire when student soldiers practiced with field artillery and live ammunition overlooking Cayuga Lake. The field artillery unit was established in 1919–20 and featured 88 horses and eight guns, two of which were 155 mm. caliber. This photo is dated May 1929.

Cornell Cadet Corps

World War I combatants. They gar-
nered a front-page banner headline in
The New York Herald of May 26,
1917: "Cornell Boys First at Front
with Stars and Stripes." In that year,
the Cornell Cadet Corps became the
Reserve Officer Training Corps
(ROTC). Within two months of the
U.S. entry to World War I, 2,054 students and 128 staff members had
joined the army or navy or taken work
in an indispensable war industry. Overall, some 7,000 Cornellians were in
military uniform. About 1,500
were still in officer training programs
when the Great War ended. Cornell
provided 4,598 commissioned officers
to the effort, the most of any American civilian institution. Cornellians
received 526 decorations and citations. Sadly, 264 Cornellians perished
in the conflict. Their names may be
found in the Memorial Room on the
ground floor of the old Army Tower
(Lyon Hall), along with the battle
flags carried by Cornell units. Names
of the war dead also are carved in
stone panels of the War Memorial
Cloister (erected in 1930), which joins
the towers. Some forty rooms in the

Army and Navy Towers (Lyon and
McFadden Halls, built in 1930) are
inscribed in memory of World War I
individuals or groups, according to the
Cornell Alumni News, April 16, 1936.
A brief biography of each person
killed, along with information about
all 8,851 Cornellians who served, may
be found in the *Military Records of
Cornell University in the World War*
(1930).

peers. Cornell also provides high-powered lectures and educational tours and activities for the occasion.

As Romeyn Berry observed, "But class reunions amend all, restore balances, deflate the bumptious, re-establish a more accurate sense of relative values, and sometimes remind the thoughtless that the University continues to be an influence in their lives long after it has sent them forth misbranded as a finished product . . . it takes no more than a single June twilight on the Library slope, the music of bells, a single soft night under the stars in nostalgic surroundings, to work a complete cure for all that ever ails alumni. . . . After middle life the bifocals are slow in picking up the names on the buttons which are falsely supposed to identify old friends. It's hard to recognize in stylish stouts, in ponderous executives, the same lissome youths who once kicked a goal, or took third place in the broad jump, or showed an unsuspected sprinting ability in escaping the clutches of the Ithaca Gestapo" (Berry, 1950, p. 154).

Today, tents on the ag, arts, and engineering quads are likely to tell passersby that class reunion fever has returned, with particular focus on classes celebrating five-year and decade increments. Reunion traditionally is a time to cruise, schmooze, and booze with former classmates, to swap real and imagined stories about the good old days, and to infer indirectly how one is progressing in life, through inevitable self-comparisons with one's

AGRICULTURE QUADRANGLE

The "Big Four" on the agriculture quadrangle were all constructed in time to welcome the Ford Model-T era, as shown in this John P. Troy image. Stone Hall (center), Roberts Hall (right, center), and East Roberts Hall (far right), built from 1905–06, are now gone, making way for today's Kennedy Hall and the new Roberts Hall. The first Home Economics building, later called Comstock Hall (left) when it was occupied by the Department of Entomology, was built in 1912.

Stone Hall was named for John Lemuel Stone, class of 1874 and a professor in the College of Agriculture. Over the years it housed departments such as agronomy, farm practice, botany, rural education, and education. It also housed the ag college library until Mann Library opened in 1953.

Roberts Hall was named for Isaac Phillips Roberts, director of the college from 1874–1903. Over the years, it housed administrative, business, and extension offices, as well as such departments as Communication Arts, Entomology, Floriculture, Limnology, Pomology, and Ornithology. The roof antennas were associated with the Department of Meteorology, which cooperated with the United States Weather Bureau, forming the Central New York State Station.

East Roberts housed the dairy building and the Department of Dairy Industry for many years.

Comstock was the center of home economics at the time this photo was taken. The Computing and Communications Center now occupies the remodeled building. A portion of the old Minns Garden is glimpsed at lower left.

The contemporary image shows Kennedy Hall (near foreground) and the new Roberts Hall (left, background), first occupied in March 1990. Also glimpsed are Warren Hall (beyond the far transportation kiosk, light-colored brick) and Plant Science (right). Kennedy Hall houses the Departments of Communication, Education, and Landscape Architecture, as well as the David L. Call Auditorium and the Trillium dining facility (dark brick, center right). Roberts Hall contains the administration of the College of Agriculture and Life Sciences, the Agricultural Experiment Station administration, and offices of Cornell Cooperative Extension. Warren Hall, built in 1933 and named in honor of George F. Warren, department head of Agricultural Economics and Farm Management from 1908–38, houses the Departments of Applied Economics and Management, Rural Sociology, and Biometrics. A number of domestic and international agricultural and community development institutes and programs also are housed in Warren Hall. Plant Sciences, built in 1931, houses the departments of Plant Biology, Plant Pathology, and Horticulture.

STONE HALL & ROBERTS HALL, AND ROBERTS HALL & KENNEDY HALL

A late-1920s image of Stone and Roberts Halls, taken from Bailey Hall and looking southeast toward Schoellkopf Crescent and Schoellkopf Memorial Hall, gives a misleading impression of a sleepy campus, the abandoned road prone to dust devils. The number of automobiles, however, suggests a crowd somewhere on the Ag Quad.

The contemporary image shows Roberts Hall (near foreground) and Kennedy Hall (right, behind trees). The curved roof of the fourth floor of Roberts Hall provides a spacious, well-lit studio area for the Department of Landscape Architecture.

ROBERTS BARN & COMPUTING AND COMMUNICATIONS CENTER

On the site of the present Computing and Communications Center (opposite), responsible for campus access to the Internet, e-mail, and other communication technologies and software, once stood "Roberts' Barn," a nickname for the structure designed by Frank Ayres Wright in 1877, then built and operated under the direction of Isaac Phillips Roberts, Cornell's first dean of the College of Agriculture. Roberts, who had spent his boyhood in East Varick, Seneca County, on the western shores of Cayuga Lake, joined Cornell after a successful career as a carpenter, school teacher, and farmer in New York, Indiana, and Iowa. Immediately before joining Cornell in 1874, Roberts worked as superintendent of the College Farm at Iowa State College of Agriculture and Mechanic Arts, Ames. Roberts wrote of his Iowa State experience: "I had begun to lose faith in the college method of raising the business of farming to an intelligent and dignified calling . . . but my trusted friend said, 'go to Cornell—it is an opportunity which comes to man but once in a lifetime'— . . . And so I set out not knowing whither I was

going. . . . When I went to Cornell the farm buildings consisted of a small, dilapidated farm house and several low, rambling barns. . . . Of necessity the initial undertakings were very small; and the Agricultural Department shared the contempt heaped upon the University as a 'freshwater,' 'hayseed' affair. . . . It was not until 1880 that the 'model barn' [also called the "universal barn," the "north barn" and "Roberts' Barn"] was erected . . . an L-shaped structure . . . 128 feet long and 120 feet broad—when the piggery was added later, 140 feet broad—and like the Dutchman's horse, 'the biggest the way you measured it last.' The lower story was devoted to the dairy animals and from their feet to the top of the metal cow surmounting the lightning rod which projected about four feet above the cupola, was just one hundred feet. The basement also contained a covered yard, an engine and boiler, an ice house, a root cellar and a milk delivery room. The horses, wagons, granaries and office occupied most of the second floor; the sheep, grain, hay, straw and stationary thresher, the third floor.

The mows would hold the sheaves of 600 to 700 bushels of grain and 100 tons of hay. Provision was made for everything a barn should contain except poultry—which it should not contain" (Roberts, 1946, p. 124).

Roberts was responsible for a new approach to farming, which involved practical, trial-and-error field experiments and, increasingly, the scientific method. In an angle of his model barn, for example, he constructed " . . . a great cavernous silo of concrete with a provision for two huge screws by which silage could be pressed down solidly" (ibid., p. 127). Roberts believed this was only the second such structure in the United States that was constructed for the purpose of preserving green roughage for livestock. Various approaches were attempted, sometimes resulting in half-rotten, smelly silage. He finally succeeded in his preservation efforts, with the help of a galvanized, airtight iron cylinder, filled with green corn and carbonic acid, a deadly gas. Triumphantly, "when the material came out it was apparently in just the same state as when it went in" (ibid.). This method,

however, eventually proved too expensive. Just the same, Roberts demonstrated that the farmer need not be helpless, resigned to tradition-bound deterministic fate; new, tested methods would produce superior practices. Roberts became the first director of the Cornell University Agricultural Experiment Station, established by Congress in March 1887, thus formalizing his leadership over a process of scientific experimentation and research publication that benefited the citizens of New York State (and farmers everywhere). Dean Roberts, who labored at Cornell from 1874 through June 1903, is remembered as "The Father of Agricultural Science."

This concentration often led to outside misapprehension of Cornell, as noted by Founder's Day speaker James Morgan Hart: "Now there is one truth concerning this university which should be proclaimed from the house-tops, the truth that of all our American institutions of learning Cornell is the one which has been most persistently misunderstood, even by its friends. Its enemies sneer at it as a farm with a blacksmith shop. We, of course, find

the jibe too poor to call forth even a smile. Yet few of us have grasped and lived up to the truth that this is indeed a university, an institution which teaches all subjects, so far as its means may suffice" (Hart, 1913, p. 12).

Once a year, in cooperation with the Department of Animal Science, students bring a cow to the Ag Quad to play a fund-raising game of "cow-chip bingo." The animal is placed in a pen, the area marked off in squares. Interested faculty, administrators, staff, students, and others buy a square. Any square that is the recipient of a cow chip wins part of the proceeds. Today, that's as close as cows get to the location that once had plenty of cows and where every square was a winner, often.

The Computing and Communications Center, housed in a remodeled and renamed Comstock Hall (originally constructed in 1912 for home economics use), stands on the site of the old Roberts Barn. Today, CCC plays an increasingly vital role on campus, containing a variety of offices including the Academic Technology Center, Academic Computing Services, the Office of Information Technologies, Center for Learning and Teaching, University Counsel, and Board of Trustees offices.

A different building named Comstock Hall, used since 1986, stands on Garden Avenue east of Barton Hall and Industrial and Labor Relations. Comstock Hall houses the Department of Entomology, a field that John Henry Comstock (1849–1931) and his spouse, Anna Botsford Comstock (1854–1930), helped develop at Cornell. Anna Botsford Comstock '86 was "one of America's twelve outstanding women" during her lifetime (Bishop, 1962, p. 301). Comstock Hall also is the headquarters of Biological Sciences (courses 101–104), Media and Technology Services (print media, television and satellite, video conferencing, and so on), as well as University Photography.

CENTRAL HEATING PLANT

Central heating was not a part of Cornell for decades. In the early period of building construction, provision was made for independent heating. For example, Cascadilla Hall, which predated the University, required each student and faculty room to heat with coal independently. President White, who truly disliked Cascadilla, was deathly afraid of fire, knowing full well that an individual's momentary carelessness might lead to disaster for all. Morris Bishop wrote: "[In Cascadilla Hall] the provident lived in a constant terror of fire; White and others equipped themselves with coiled rope ladders. . . . As for heat, one may judge by the experience of a Russian student in January, 1869. He put his high Russian boots outside his door, apparently in the expectation that they would be polished. A whimsical student filled them with water; and in the morning they were frozen solid" (Bishop, 1962, pp. 92–93).

Nor was Cascadilla the only source of President White's concern. The buildings first built by the University—Morrill, White, and McGraw—"were the reverse of fireproof. A south

wind was likely to blow ashes down the chimneys and out onto the floors" (ibid., p. 96). Some students resided in Morrill and White. In White's report for February 1869, other sources of possible conflagration were causes for alarm: " . . . he points out that in Morrill Hall thirty-two dormitory stoves are under the care of students, and four stoves and four furnaces are tended by assistants. The students have in their rooms about fifty kerosene lamps, one of which has already exploded. And there was no water available" (ibid., p. 96).

McGraw Hall was built with its own central heating but was so frigid that a sympathetic faculty member shared

The contemporary view shows a second smokestack, added in 1927. The platform halfway up the smokestack on the right provided the vantage point from which the panorama on pages 78–79 was photographed.

The building is located south of Dryden Road (NYS Route 366), between the intersection of Dryden with Hoy Road to the west and the intersection with Pine Tree Road to the east. Today it is a combined heat and electric power plant that provides heat to nearly all central campus and residential halls, or a combined 10 million square feet. More than one billion pounds of steam heat annually are generated by natural gas and oil in addition to coal. The plant also provides nearly 15 percent of the campus electricity requirements at about half the fuel input of a conventional electric power plant.

with President White a student's complaint about the cold, scrawled on the bottom of an examination essay. While it must have been difficult to write an examination under those conditions, for safety reasons alone it made sense to provide the entire campus with a central heating source.

Although the Central Heating Plant will never be pointed out by tour guides as a key campus sight, its construction was a major campus event. It nears completion in this December 15, 1922, photograph by John P. Troy. The single smokestack would soon belch smoke from the coal being delivered along the railway trestle in the background.

STONE ARCH BRIDGE

President White recalled in his 1905 *Autobiography* just how difficult getting to and around campus was in its earliest days. On the University's opening, October 7, 1868, he described how he put on a brave face, but inwardly felt fearful, anxious, and depressed: " . . . university buildings [were] unready and the grounds unkempt . . . all that part of our domain was then a ragged corn-field surrounded by rail fences" (White, 1905, p. 344). The grounds, littered with piles of soil and waste construction materials, were muddy due to the wet autumn that year. The commonly used route to Morrill Hall, the sole, but uncompleted building, was up East Hill from the village, through the cemetery and along cow paths through the pastures. There was no southern entrance. That there was no permanent bridge across Cascadilla gorge was an obvious disadvantage, given that most of the students and faculty lived in Cascadilla Hall on the south side and the University was being built on the north side. Various temporary wooden bridges were constructed, but they eventually col-

lapsed. This permanent stone arch bridge finally spanned Cascadilla gorge in 1896. Generations of Cornellians, their families, and friends have used the bridge since without giving it much thought. We can forgive them that; especially on Graduation Day, there are other things to think about.

"The lines and stage directions have been changed with the years, but the act itself remains essentially the same. Commencement still ends everything; starts anything. There's still the momentary heart-gripping— an instant of poignant recollection and misgiving—when the Danby peaks shut off the view of the towers and Lake for all time"

(Berry, 1950, p. 154).

CASCADILLA GORGE

No University buildings are found in Cascadilla gorge. A number of bridges span the creek, however, beginning with the Fish Hatchery Bridge at the east edge of the main campus, followed by the Judd Falls Bridge, the bridge for Dryden Road (NYS 366), the GEV Synchrotron Service Bridge, the Dwyer Dam Bridge, the Eddy Dam Footbridge, the Trolley Footbridge, the Central Avenue Stone Arch Bridge, and the Stewart Avenue Bridge at the west edge of the main campus. Perhaps the best-known of these bridges is the Stone Arch Bridge, from which this

photograph was taken. It was built in 1896 with funding by William Henry Sage (son of early benefactor Henry Williams Sage). Stone Arch Bridge links Collegetown's Central Avenue northward to the Ho Plaza and the central campus, leading to Jennie McGraw Tower, Uris Library, and the John M. Olin Library. The late spring snowfalls in this gorge are especially scenic as seen in this Stone Arch Bridge western view. Little has changed over the years, except that a larger apartment complex has replaced a smaller structure on the Collegetown edge of the gorge, and a petite gazebo belonging to Lambda Chi Alpha fraternity, 125 Edgemoor Lane, is now visible on Cornell's West Campus edge. The gazebo

"Streams flowing into the lake have cut deep channels in the soft Portage sandstone of the hills and tumble through the chasms in many waterfalls. Two gorges, those of Fall Creek and Cascadilla Creek, are on the borders of the campus. . . . Cascadilla Creek is smaller than Fall Creek and has carved its gorge less deeply. It descends its ravine in a series of rapids and cascades.

—Guide to the Campus of Cornell University, 1920

offers a peaceful vista for the fraternity, founded in 1909 and installed at Cornell in 1913.

President A. D. White himself is said to have designed the walks along Cascadilla gorge, best accessed spring through fall. Winter's snow and ice make the walk dangerous, given the depth of the gorge itself.

CASCADILLA GORGE & EDDY DAM FOOTBRIDGE

The campus always has required bridges—stone arches, steel bridges, suspension bridges, wooden bridges. Most have been utilitarian and help get the work of the day done. Others have provided solace and are primarily restorative to the human spirit. These photographs, taken at the Eddy Dam Footbridge in Cascadilla Gorge, show that the latter type of bridge was and is very much in vogue. Melissa S. Groo, research assistant with the Cornell Laboratory of Ornithology, is shown in the contemporary photograph with her dog, Ernie, an Australian shepherd mix.

COLLEGETOWN

Southeast of the Sheila W. and Richard J. Schwartz Center for the Performing Arts, where Sheldon Court now stands near the College Avenue intersection with Dryden Road, there once was a small body of water known as "Willow Pond." Otis Eddy used the water to power his cotton mill until 1866. For a while, after nearby Cascadilla Hall became the first student and faculty residence hall, a hydraulic ram was installed to pump water from the pond into the building. It was so often out of order, however, that University officials were forced to provide outdoor privies for the use of the inhabitants. College Avenue, then known as Heustis Street, was lined with Victorian houses, whose owners often offered room and board services to students. A wooden bridge traversed the inlet to the pond. Water-loving, coppiced willow trees grew vigorously on the banks. This photograph dates from the 1890s.

Today, a commercial scene occupies the site, the pond long since drained and the site filled. The once tranquil location hums with pedestrian and vehicular traffic, and businesses such as Collegetown Bagels, Student Agencies Properties, Bear Necessities, Sam Goody, and Collegetown Convenience Store cater to students and campus visitors. The "VC" banner hanging from the nearest building refers to "Victory Club," an annual casino night and charity ball held to benefit worthy organizations and causes, such as the American Red Cross and the World Trade Center Disaster Fund. Hundreds of tux-clad Cornellians participate as James Bond wannabes in the Alpha Delta Phi–sponsored event, which *Playboy* magazine once called "the best party in the Ivy League."

Farther down College Avenue stood the proud Phi Kappa Psi fraternity house at 71 Heustis Avenue, shown in this photo taken during the fall of 1886, the year the building was constructed. In 1899 it became the Delta Chi chapter house after Phi Kappa Psi moved to 1 McGraw Place. In 1900, the building was destroyed by fire. Two brick buildings were later constructed on the site and served as a billiard hall and the Fire Company Number Nine station.

Today, the scene features Dino's Café & Grill, 313 College Avenue, purveyor of grill specialties, pizza, and bar beverages, and The Nines, 311 College Avenue, featuring deep-dish pizza and live entertainment. Both are part of the vibrant Collegetown scene. The present Phi Kappa Psi is located at 525 Stewart Avenue.

MILLER-HELLER HOUSE

The Miller-Heller house, built on land bought from Ezra Cornell at 122 Eddy Street, was constructed in 1876 by William Henry Miller, early Cornell and Ithaca architect, as his personal residence. Edgar Dethlefsen, Miller's biographer, described the residence as "modest but architecturally unique." Miller (1848–1922) was the first student to enroll for architectural studies under Charles Babcock as part of Cornell's inaugural class of 1868. While at Cornell, Miller studied mathematics, science, English, French, German, mechanics, and drafting, all to supplement his earlier two years of study at Clinton Liberal Institute. He remained in Ithaca to practice his profession from 1872 until his death in 1922, employing Romanesque arches, towers, and elements of Queen Anne style. In Tompkins County, about seventy buildings are attributed to his firm. Miller helped design the A. D. White President's House (when he was in his 20s and a college student) and later, the house's south wing addition. A close personal friendship grew between Miller and White, who had "an avid interest in the arts and in

architecture," according to Dethlefsen. During Miller's career as architect, he also designed residences for several other Cornell notables, including Henry W. Sage, John McGraw, Jennie McGraw Fiske and Willard Fiske, the Bela MacKoon house (later the residence of Jacob Gould Schurman, third president of Cornell), and a number of houses for Cornell professors, including Thomas Frederick Crane and Albert N. Prentiss. Among Miller's many campus designs were Barnes Hall (1889), Boardman Hall (1891–92), the Andrew Dickson White Memorial Gateway at Eddy Street (1896), Prudence Risley Residential College (1913), Stimson Hall (1901–02) and Uris Library (1889–90). Miller also was a furniture designer and interior decorator.

His residence at 122 Eddy Street featured simple wooden panels in the ceilings and molding that were combined with wall hangings of brocade, canvas, and other materials. According to Dethlefsen, the "elegantly simple" home was furnished with antiques and featured stained glass panels, "a large bubbles," and an Arabic frieze. The structure "was the recipient of his constant attention and was designed and redesigned to house his family (wife Emma Halsey and four children) and an extensive collection of art objects, and his musical instruments" (Dethlefsen, 1957, p. 2). Among the musical instruments was an in-house organ.

After the Millers left the residence, it was used for many years as a student boarding house (nicknamed "The Asylum") under the supervision of "Warden" Lillian P. Heller, during the period when the historical photograph on page 114 was taken by C. Hadley Smith. A scrapbook of the hijinks, parties, and daily lives of the students who lived there was kept for a number of years by the residents. Each year's entry was given an appropriate title, such as *Insanity Runs in Our Family (by the Inmates 1944–45), Who's Zoo in 122 (1948–49), Events and Personalities Behind the Dark, Green Walls of the Chateau d'Heller, (1950–51),* and *The Polyglots (1954–55).* Included are vivid descriptions, poems, cartoons, and photographs that chronicle such topics as the Asylum's Constitution, systems of fines for misdemeanors such as sleeping through meals or not cleaning the "cells" (apartments), the care and feeding of the cantankerous coal furnace, a 1946 guestroom fire due to an iron left on, dealing with a "ripe" mouse that had gone into an inaccessible crawl space to die, building snowmen and snowwomen, a maple syrup "sugaring-off" party hosted by Mrs. Heller, unusual recipes tried by neophyte cooks, the intramural basketball record of the Asylum team (University independent league

champs in 1945–46!), an autographed guest list for a holiday party that reveals a virtual United Nations at Cornell, and touching tributes to Lillian Heller, as well as an account of her adventures in feeding her furry and feathered friends and winning awards at the New York Flower Show. Ownership transferred to the University in 1957 after Mrs. Heller's death. Presently, the building and grounds are used by the College of Architecture, Art and Planning for visitors and guests, as well as for social events and receptions.

In Romeyn Berry's view, "Looking back through the changes that four decades have brought about, one can see now that a useful piece of social machinery went out with the passing of the student boarding-houses. Some of them were pretty squalid, of course, but from the moment you signed up and were given a fixed place at a big table, you became part of the social fabric of Cornell. . . . Not infrequently, your friendships, and the little niche you were to fill at the University, were determined at your first meal" (Berry, 1950, pp. 39–40).

CASCADILLA HALL

The tentative site of Cornell University, as it was being discussed and debated in Albany in the early 1860s, was Ezra Cornell's cow pasture. A. D. White, then a fellow legislator who worked with Ezra Cornell to secure passage of enabling legislation, at first urged that Syracuse be the host community. But Ezra Cornell was a stubborn man. He knew that Ithaca, with its beautiful views, was the right spot. Getting his way in this case, however, led to a problem—what would the University do for classrooms, laboratories, administrative offices, and residences for students and faculty and their families?

Work began on campus buildings, at first called No. 1 and No. 2, and then North and South Hall, and finally Morrill Hall and White Hall, as soon as it was determined there would be a Cornell University on the cow pasture. (Incidentally, President A. D. White wanted the lower portion of Libe Slope, where the West Campus residences now stand, to be the site of the academic buildings, while Cornell wanted the upper brow of the library slope.) No. 1 and No. 2 would solve most of the educational space and infrastructure issues. But residences?

Fortunately, there was Cascadilla Place. Ezra Cornell had suffered from typhus fever in 1847. He attributed his recovery to hydropathy, which relied upon water cures (such as drinking mineral water and taking cold-water baths) in treating disease. When Miss Samantha Nivison sought backers for her plans in 1863 to offer a water cure in Ithaca and to train women as nurses and physicians, Ezra Cornell became the major stockholder in the investment of erecting a sanatorium for that purpose. Cascadilla Place was located on the southern edge of Cascadilla gorge, at the place where Otis Eddy operated a cotton mill in earlier days, and for whom Ezra Cornell worked as a mechanic beginning in 1828. The building never went into operation as originally intended. Instead, it served as the major campus residence for the new student body and faculty and their families, becoming the hub of a closely knit Cornell extended family that commingled official and social interactions.

Goldwin Smith wrote, "Cascadilla held us all at first. The old pile claims our veneration as the cradle of University life. . . . Life in it was perhaps not very luxurious; but it was very social. The sight of it recalls to my memory many pleasant evenings and many a game of euchre. My thoughts often revert to my rooms in Cascadilla and to the platform from which I used to gaze on sunsets more gorgeous than those of my native land [Great Britain], and sometimes to watch the eagle hovering over the lake" (Smith, 1904, pp. 10–11).

Travel between Cascadilla Place and the new academic buildings was by no means easy. A wooden bridge across the gorge had just been completed the day before the campus opened. Slippery and muddy trails were the rule rather than the exception. Paths were rarely level in an era before major landscaping had been accomplished. Students arriving on campus from the village below took the "Bone-Yard Cut," a shortcut that wound uphill north of Cascadilla Creek through the village cemetery. By 1876 an omnibus transportation system catered to students living on the village flats, making the half-hour climb up East Hill to Cascadilla from the Clinton House six times a day. A sense of raw adventure must have been experienced by the first 412 students, (including 332 freshmen) admitted to this untried and untested institution, which was still hanging doors on hinges and trying to figure out how to plumb the buildings.

In Romeyn Berry's view, "When Cornell was officially opened in the fall of 1868, Morrill Hall and White were still unfinished. But Cascadilla Place was a going concern from the start, prepared to handle all the starry-eyed students, all the professors, that could get to Ithaca by rail or steamboat, by stagecoach or canal packet. The main floor then held the offices of the first President, Andrew Dickson White (1865–85), the Registrar, and the Military Commandant, together with the general business office. There were here, also, two lecture rooms and the eating establishment. . . . The three upper stories contained apartments for professors and their families and many rooms for students . . . in what must have been the utmost squalor, for,

Cascadilla Hall

apart from water taps in the chilly halls, the sanitary arrangements were all out of doors on the other side of the road. The place echoed all day, and a good part of the night, to the cries of complaining babies, the ribald shouts of whiskered students, and the brilliant conversations of Goldwin Smith and Teefy Crane, of George William Curtis and Louis Agassiz, Jimmy Hart, James Russell Lowell, John Stanton Gould, Bayard Taylor, and Theodore Dwight" (Berry, 1950, p. 2).

President White referred to Cascadilla Place as an "ill-ventilated, ill-smelling, uncomfortable, ill-looking almshouse." Water was drawn by bucket from a campus well. Toilets were tended with dirt and chemicals. No baths were available, although one of the first students, John Yawger Davis, wrote to his brother, Charles, in Auburn on October 9, 1868, that "when things are more settled we will have a bathing room in each hall where we can take a shower bath either hot or cold or get water to wash ourselves whenever we wish." An investigation of the sanitary conditions in 1881, however, showed the building

was still "an unholy, unsanitary mess" (Parsons, 1968, p. 101).

The early view of Cascadilla Hall at far left, clad with ivy and fire escapes, also offers a glimpse of the electric railway tracks that served public transportation needs. The service suggested in this photo did not help Cascadilla Hall residents until 1891–92, however, when the tracks extended up East Hill and across Cascadilla Gorge on its own wooden bridge to the Armory on the other side. In 1896, the line extended northward along East Avenue, with a shuttle branch west and parallel to Boardman Hall and the University library.

A major remodeling took place in 1913, but the contemporary view of Cascadilla Hall at the corner of Dryden Road and Eddy Street in Collegetown reveals further changes in the hall's roof and suggests the native bluestone blocks quarried nearby for the building's construction have darkened, but also proven durable. The residence hall, with all six floors recently refurbished, houses 300 to 325 students.

EDDY GATE

President White donated the 1896 structure spanning the original southern entrance to campus. It's known informally as "Eddy Gate" but officially as "The Andrew Dickson White Memorial Gateway." The most colorful and amusing name, however, is "Andy White's Chocolate Layer Cake." Designed by William Henry Miller, the gate is made of alternating courses of reddish brown Berea limestone and white Ohio sandstone, topped with an elaborate wrought-iron arch. When it was newer, it did resemble a cake with differently colored layers, and in an odd way suggested the Cornell colors of carnelian red and white.

The inscription on the gate is serious, however. President White was fond of a Latin inscription over the ancient gate at the University of Padua, in Padova, Italy, and he had it added to Eddy Gate. It reads: "So enter that daily thou mayest become more learned and thoughtful; So depart that daily thou mayest become more useful to thy country and to mankind." President White's purpose in having the gate erected was to remember all those who had worked with him to found and guide Cornell University during its early years, as well as the students who had given the young University their vote of confidence by attending courses and earning degrees. It also remains up-to-date with these words: "In Remembrance . . . with a God speed to all who . . . shall go hence to their life work with noble purpose and firm resolves. . . ."

The vintage July 1946 photograph at far left was taken for Standard Oil Company of New Jersey by renowned photographer Gordon Parks. Parks first attracted national notice after he began work as a photographer for the famed Farm Security Administration photography unit in 1942. He stayed with the FSA through its absorption into the Office of War Information in 1943 and soon thereafter was assigned as a war correspondent with the African-American 99th Pursuit Squadron, 332nd Fighter Group. He rejoined FSA/OWI boss Roy Stryker at Standard Oil of New Jersey in 1944, before the end of World War II, and stayed there until 1949, when he joined *Life* magazine as the first African-American photographer on staff. In Parks's photo, two businesses down Eddy Street in the background were the Eddygate Restaurant and the Red & White store.

The contemporary scene shows a few outward changes downhill. Dunbar's (favorite watering hole of ice-hockey aficionados), Gnomon Copy Service, and Fontana's Shoe Sales and Repair stand where the restaurant and grocery store once were located. Also, there's ivy on the gate pillars, a stop sign to slow traffic, smaller trees, more power lines, and the newer buildings are larger and of brick construction rather than wood.

COSMOPOLITAN CLUB

The Cosmopolitan Club was established in 1904 to foster fellowship among all nationalities of students attending Cornell and to serve as an international clearinghouse for ideas. Twenty-one nationalities were listed in the charter membership. The global nature of its founding is reflected in the fact that it took Professor Goldwin Smith's phrase as its motto—"Above all nations is humanity." A residence was built for international students in 1910–11 at 301 Bryant Avenue. This photo of the Cosmopolitan Club in 1933 demonstrates the pride with which international students displayed the flags of the residents' home countries.

In recent years, the building has operated as an apartment complex with five floors, thirty rooms, and fifty tenants. While it no longer functions solely as an international house, the role of the University as an international crossroads has ballooned. At the turn of the twenty-first century, 3,024 international students were attending Cornell (15.9 percent of all students), with 1,044 studying at the undergraduate level for a total of 7.7 percent of

all undergraduates. The 1,980 international graduate students represented 36.6 percent of all graduate students enrolled. One hundred twenty-four countries were represented, with large contingents from Canada, the People's Republic of China, South Korea, India, Singapore, Japan, Taiwan, Hong Kong, Thailand, and Turkey. These students added a cosmopolitan flavor to "centrally isolated" Ithaca, whether from Albania or Zimbabwe. Those from the Solomon Islands, Burkina Faso, Uzbekistan, the Union of Myanmar, Azerbaijan, St. Lucia, Bhutan, and Oman, and most of the other countries no doubt had plenty of opportunities to educate others about their homes and cultures. Central gathering places for international students these days are Caldwell Hall (1913) on the Ag Quad, where the International Students and Scholars Office is found, as well as the Mario Einaudi Center for International Studies in Uris Hall.

LLENROC & DELTA PHI

Over the years, Ezra Cornell and his family had lived in relatively modest quarters. Toward the end of his life, the founder began to think of yet another major building project. This would be a home unlike any other in Ithaca. According to Kermit Parsons, it was a mansion of impressive dimensions, "solid, rich, and somewhat ostentatious." It would be located west of Stewart Avenue, downhill on Cornell Avenue toward University Avenue. Ezra Cornell began construction of his post-Civil War Gothic home in 1867, and it was completed in 1875, a year after his death. His wife, Mary, and her daughters were to live in the house for 32 years, however. It was sold to Delta Phi fraternity in 1911.

A. D. White wrote, "[Ezra Cornell] visited several quarries . . . to choose the best possible building-stone, he employed some German stone-carvers who had recently left work upon the Cathedral of Cologne, brought them to Ithaca, and allowed them to work on with no interference save from the architect. If they gave a month or more to the carving of a single capital or corbel, he made no remonstrance.

When he had thus secured the best stone-work he selected the best seasoned oak and walnut and called skillful carpenters from England. In thus going abroad for artisans there was no want of loyalty to his countrymen, nor was there any alloy of vanity in his motives. His purpose evidently was to erect a house (Llenroc) which should

White suggested the words to be carved on the stone scroll, or ribbon, at Llenroc's front entrance, a translation of the old German motto "Treu und Fest" (True and Firm). Although the building also was called "Villa Cornell" and "Cornell's Folly" (due to its cost and proximity to the cemetery), Ezra Cornell took the jibes in good humor, noting in his spare Quaker manner that the neighborhood was peaceful at least.

After it was purchased by Delta Phi fraternity, it became known by the Llenroc name (Cornell spelled backward). The fraternity brothers have taken great pride in maintaining the property, a national historic landmark, and in the early 1980s had insured the antique lead-crystal chandeliers for $500,000 each. The chandelier in the front hall reportedly incorporates one of five original prototype bronze casts for the Statue of Liberty, rejected because the figurine's arm is bare.

be as perfect a specimen of the builder's art as he could make it, and therefore useful, as an example of thoroughly good work, to the local workmen" (White, 1905, pp. 323–324).

McGRAW-FISKE MANSION &
CHI PSI

A smoldering love that blazed briefly but ended in an early death; the fire that destroyed the lovers' private mansion and took the lives of four students and three Ithaca volunteer firemen; the bad blood of a seven-year legal battle that pitted the bereaved husband against the University over his wife's will and fortune, initially leaving injured feelings and enmity all around, but ending well; these are the themes that form the legend of Jennie McGraw and Daniel Willard Fiske. The truth depends upon which version of the story is told by what biased weaver of tales. We have relied on a touching and sympathetic account of the unfortunate couple (Williams, 1949).

Jennie McGraw was the only child of wealthy Cornell University benefactor John McGraw. Born September 14, 1840, in Dryden, New York, she was the apple of her father's eye and he was her "dear one" and "Pa." He was twice a millionaire in his early 40s and while he married three times, Jennie was the one constant woman in his household. It is said he scared off many potential suitors for her attractive and gracious daughter's hand. Like her father, Jennie took a keen interest in Cornell University's development, and considerable money flowed through her purse to the institution on the hill. She was sickly, struck with the same disease—tuberculosis, scourge of the times—that had caused her mother's death when Jennie was only seven years of age. Her life was one of intellect and appreciation for the arts, particularly music. Increasingly, as her father's health worsened, she took over the management of his financial affairs and lumber business.

Daniel Willard Fiske was born November 11, 1831, in Ellisburg, New York. He was a brilliant man, gifted in language and literature, a noted bibliophile who specialized in Icelandic sagas and literature, Rhaeto-Romanic literature, Dante, Petrarch, chess, geography, journalism, and international diplomacy. He was among the first faculty members to join Cornell and served as University librarian. He was friend to the celebrated scholar and lecturer Bayard Taylor and belonged to the same English club as American author Henry James. He associated with Danish author Hans Christian Andersen and British poet laureate Sir Alfred Austin. Mark Twain wrote that "he was as dear and sweet a soul as I have ever known."

Willard Fiske apparently loved Jennie McGraw from the first time he met her in 1869. He wrote a poem concerning her on that occasion, saying (in small part), "My soul is drifting so fast, so fast, From doubt and dark to love and light." For the next dozen years, most of them spent in secret love, Fiske would write an average of five heartfelt poems a year about Jennie and his feelings toward her. He showed them to no one for most of that time.

In 1875 Jennie traveled to Europe for pleasure, but while there suffered the beginnings of a more severe form of her illness. Back in Ithaca, Professor Fiske, smoldering and suffering in silence, kept writing poetry: "I feel the more that thou art mine—Though no sad sigh Thine ear did hear, no loving sign Thine eye espy."

Jennie returned. John McGraw died, and Jennie took over the business. Fiske wrote a eulogy honoring her father, which he shared with her after their acquaintanceship had grown measurably. Increasingly, her health failed. Seeking a climate that would ease her cough and slow her increasing weakness, she finally dispersed the belongings of her Ithaca home by auction in March 1878, before leaving again for Europe and Tsarist Russia. She intended to return to Ithaca, however, instructing architect William Henry Miller concerning her ideas for a new mansion. Miller made plans for "a towered, gabled pile . . . of Ohio sandstone, the interior paneled in various fine woods, each room designed for a special function . . . without doubt, one of the finest private dwellings in the entire state of New York . . . a sumptuous mansion" (ibid., p. 51). The mansion began to take shape with construction in April 1880 on a 30-acre site with magnificent views of Ithaca and Cayuga Lake.

Jennie's illness advanced. She met up with Professor Fiske again after he broke off his studies of Runic literature in Iceland and checked into the same Rome hotel where Jennie was staying.

Earlier, he had discussed his feelings about Jennie with President Andrew D. White, then serving as a diplomat in Germany. With White's encouragement bolstering his nerve, Fiske finally confessed to Jennie that he loved her, and asked her to marry him. Jennie assented. His poetry soared. He declared he did not see "Caesar City's streets," but had eyes only for her: "Only this I see—Close by my side one sweetly-smiling face, Long sought, now found, and to be sought no more."

Jennie's illness, although she hopefully imagined it was improving with each change in scenery, continued to worsen. Her coughing and hemorrhages increased. A thorough medical examination in Berlin on July 1, 1880, yielded an ominous report concerning the state of her lungs. With this news, President A. D. White and her own legal counsel advised that she and Professor Fiske be married immediately. They exchanged vows on July 14. Some who did not know of his long love for her were suspicious that he was an unscrupulous fortune hunter. The truth was exactly the opposite.

Professor Fiske had long avoided displaying his affection to Jennie out of deference to her father, her wealth, and her station in life. Immediately before the wedding, he signed a prenuptial agreement that renounced his rights to his wife's fortune, which he might have realized under Prussian marriage laws. He declined Jennie's suggestion that he nullify this agreement and refused to look over her will when she offered to show it to him. He was not marrying her for her money.

After the wedding they traveled widely for her health and to buy furnishings and art for the Ithaca mansion. They finally ended up in Egypt, where doctors thought her health might rebound. On a splendid voyage on the Nile "Will," as Jennie now referred to him, showed her his cache of passionate poetry, which he had written so lovingly to her over the preceding decade. She was touched and quickly memorized several favorites. Soon after, fever and hot weather made Jennie's life absolutely miserable and she lapsed into a semicoma for several days. They retreated to Italy.

The passage was stormy, and Jennie arrived exhausted. They pressed on to Venice where Jennie wrote of Will— "the dearest of men, so considerate, so very unselfish. He is very cheerful, makes always the best of everything" (ibid., p. 64). But Will was only too aware of his wife's precarious condition. Their hope was to return to Ithaca, but he worried about the effects of the long ocean voyage on Jennie's condition. They finally sailed in September 1881.

The Ithaca mansion stood ready for the couple. The man who met the Fiskes at the lighthouse harbor on the lake in Ithaca described the scene: "Mrs. Fiske was sick, awful sick, and they had her propped up on pillows. I drove them up the hill. . . . We went right by the mansion that had been built for them to live in. Mrs. Fiske raised up from her pillows, looked at it and said: 'It surpasses all my expectations'" (ibid., p. 65). A month later, at the age of 41, Jennie Fiske died in Fiske's bachelor campus cottage, which was located immediately north of the President's House. (Willard Fiske had occupied the cottage since

November 1871, and was the first Cornell professor to build and to live on campus.) They held her funeral service in the McGraw-Fiske mansion. On that day, Daniel Willard Fiske wrote, "I shall forever keep my remembrance of her green—an easy matter since I shall never again have the chance to cherish a remembrance so pleasant. I would not exchange the happiness of the last year and a half, mingled though much of it was with the sadness of a coming grief, for the largest of fortunes. . . . I loved her . . . how much she loved me. Heaven bless her dear memory!" (ibid., p. 66)

Jennie's will remembered many people and many good causes and left a handsome sum to Cornell. Then the legal troubles began. Primarily at stake was whether or not Willard Fiske would be permitted to live in the McGraw-Fiske mansion, who would foot the bill for its upkeep, and what other University uses would be made of the building. While the case was being decided, Fiske resigned from Cornell and returned to Europe, but made provision in his will for the Cornell library to receive two-thirds of any

McGraw-Fiske Mansion & Chi Psi

amount that might accrue to him from the suit, with the remainder earmarked for payment of litigation costs. He offered the mansion to Cornell on favorable terms. President White was eager to let bygones be bygones and to accept the mansion. The board of trustees, however, declined. The litigation ended with a U.S. Supreme Court decision in favor of Willard Fiske and the McGraw family against the University's claim to the fortune.

Eventually, the mansion was acquired by Chi Psi fraternity. However, the fabled house off University Avenue was ill-fated. It was destroyed by fire on icy-cold December 7, 1906. Four of 26 fraternity brothers died as a result of the blaze, thought to have started through spontaneous combustion of varnish, floor wax, and cloth rags. The building was enveloped in flames at 3:40 A.M. The story of Cornell students' heroism in an era before fire escapes, sprinklers, and hook-and-ladder trucks, together with the deaths of three volunteer firemen due to a suddenly collapsed wall at 7 A.M., is another sad tale (see the graphic account by von Engeln, 1917).

Willard Fiske had died earlier in September 1904, in Germany, so he never knew the mansion's ultimate fate. He left the bulk of his fortune and what mattered most to him—rare book collections—to Cornell; he proved not to be a vindictive man. His remains and those of his wife now are together in the crypt at Sage Chapel, on the campus they loved so well.

A different Chi Psi building stands on the site of the former McGraw-Fiske mansion. The foundation was laid in 1907, shortly after the disastrous fire. Life goes on.

The work done by Ezra Cornell's tunnel (page 134) is readily apparent in this aerial photograph, taken in the early 1940s. Ithaca Falls dominates the picture; however, the stream running to the right of the falls is the millrace, sending diverted water through the mill area below for water power. Over the years, the primary beneficiaries of the dependable waterway and the power it supplied were the Fall Creek Milling Company, the Ithaca Gun Company, and the Reed Paper Company. Both Reed Paper and Ithaca Gun were going concerns in the early 1940s, but today, neither the mill nor the gun company exist here any longer. If they did, they would not be powered by water coursing through the tunnel and millrace to turn their mill wheels.

In the contemporary photo, the industry at the base of Lake Street has disappeared. Ithaca Gun Company, farther up on the hill, is now abandoned and vulnerable to vandalism. Very little trace of the former millrace is visible. The tunnel has declined. The University on the hill has proliferated.

Ithaca Falls

The Fall Creek gorge has refreshed many swimmers during the University's existence, as shown in this undated John P. Troy photo, although swimming there presently is strongly discouraged. The Ithaca Falls location shown in the contemporary photo, for example, is near a site relandscaped after the removal of high lead concentrations, a byproduct of the Ithaca Gun factory, now abandoned on a nearby hillside.

Ithaca Falls remains as beautiful as ever. Cornell Animal Science major Laura Diltz '03 is shown taking a photo at left.

EZRA'S TUNNEL

Ezra Cornell was born in Westchester County, New York, on January 11, 1807. After 1819, he grew up on a 150-acre "Crum Hill" farm, three miles east of De Ruyter, New York, about 41 miles in a straight line approximately northeast of Ithaca. At the age of 21, Ezra Cornell walked to Ithaca to seek his fortune. He began work as a carpenter and soon moved to work in Otis Eddy's cotton mill on Cascadilla Creek as a "mechanic and millworker," as workers with machinery were called. After a time, he left for nearby Fall Creek, where Colonel Jeremiah S. Beebe hired him to be a mechanic for his flour and plaster mills at the foot of Ithaca Falls on Fall Creek. Ezra Cornell worked out so well that he was soon managing both mills, a position he held for a dozen years.

"In the gorge of Fall Creek are many cascades and two great cataracts, the Triphammer Falls and the Ithaca Fall. Just above the Triphammer is a dam, built by the University, impounding a reservoir of about twenty acres which is called Beebe Lake, and diverting a part of the stream to the hydraulic laboratory of the college of engineering. The stream's last abrupt descent is over the Ithaca Fall, one hundred and twenty feet to the level of the valley."
—*Guide to the Campus of Cornell University,*
1920

People were attracted to the entrance of the new tunnel. More than 170 years later, they still are. Pictured are (left to right): Jeb Smith, builder and fine craftsman of Ithaca homes since 1981; Samantha Couture, '00 MFA in print-making, Department of Art; Aaron Couture, '99 Ph.D. in experimental solid state physics, and Jane Dennis, prominent Ithaca sculptor and year 2000 Ithaca Festival artist.

Ezra's Tunnel

To ensure a dependable supply of water to power the mills, Ezra Cornell planned a new millrace to run alongside Fall Creek gorge. In June 1830, workmen began blasting a tunnel above Ithaca Falls. Ezra Cornell was not quite 24 years old at the time. Over the years, the primary beneficiaries of the dependable waterway and the power it supplied were the Fall Creek Milling Company, the Ithaca Gun Company, and the Reed Paper Company.

In his biography of Ezra Cornell, Philip Dorf writes, "They made their shaft about 15 feet wide and 10 feet high, working from both ends toward the center, but on only one end at a time so as to avoid accidents. In six months the 200-foot shaft was cut through; at the center the two borings were only a few inches out of line. . . . in the spring of 1831 Cornell set about getting the water through for the use of the mills. He lowered the bed of the tunnel an additional five feet and built a new dam across the creek just below the intake gate. So pleased was Beebe with the new and unique millrace that

he ordered a plank walk built from one end of the tunnel to the other" (Dorf, 1965, p. 13).

Only the function of the tunnel has changed markedly. The Reed Paper Company was located near the bottom of the tunnel and millrace, south of Fall Creek and east of Lake Street, just below the hill northwest of the Ithaca Gun Company. As such, it would have been the most visible user (although not necessarily operating under the name of Reed Paper, because the mill had many different owners over the years), as seen from the perspective of the historic photograph on page 130.

CLASS OF '90 BOATHOUSE &
COLLYER BOATHOUSE

At its inception two major sports at Cornell University were baseball and rowing. Rowing seems an odd favorite, until one recollects that the University is "Far above Cayuga's waters with its waves of blue" and that venue, together with the Cayuga Inlet, made a long, narrow (and hence, calm) place to practice and to hold races. Professor Goldwin Smith (English History) from Great Britain also was an influence. Smith invited his friend Thomas Hughes to visit Cornell in 1870, knowing that Hughes had a favorable impression of the concept of Cornell. Hughes had written of the Institution that it was to be emulated for its "audacious combining of the practical and the cultural on an equal basis, for its . . . being Christian but not sectarian, for its admitting all but the 'idle and vicious,' and for its self-government, on a military basis" (Mack and Armytage, 1952, p. 182). More to the point, Hughes had written wildly popular fiction portraying the education of young English lads, stressing sports and leisure activities. In particular, his *Tom Brown at Oxford* (1861) spoke of rowing in glowing terms. The captain of Tom's boat, for example, was "altogether, a noble specimen of a very noble type. . . . Tall and strong of body; courageous and even-tempered; tolerant of all men; sparing of speech, but ready in action . . . he never spared himself, and was as good as three men in the boat at a pinch" (ibid., p.25). Widely read in America, Hughes was an international figure of renown and friend of Goldwin Smith's. He no doubt said something favorable about the prospects of rowing on Cayuga Lake and the Inlet when he surveyed the young Univer-

Rowing races were enormously popular with students and Ithacans, who crowded the east banks of Cayuga Lake near Stewart (Renwick) Park by the hundreds, with some more daring spectators paddling canoes and other watercraft to secure the best vantage points. An observation train, featuring bleacher-type seating in open railroad cars, also permitted the masses to witness the events and to cheer Cornellians' attempt to row to victory. O. D. von Engeln '08, assistant professor of Physical Geography, described the crowds and occasion:

"Then the crowd hurries to board the observation train for the regatta on Cayuga . . . thirty-five or more cars long, banked high with seats and crowded to capacity with a gay freight of holiday makers. . . . It winds ponderously along the shore of the lake, an engine puffing at each end. . . . Below, along the shores and on the lake . . . thousands of other spectators have been gathering for hours past, coming afoot and afloat. . . . Now the course has been cleared, the waters are oily smooth, the crews are at the start, they are off. Rhythmically, the oarsmen sway, faster forward leap the slender shells, in perfect form the Cornell crew plies the nearly invincible Courtney stroke. From the observation train, keeping just abreast of the racing eights comes a continuous roar of cheering. . . . true to form Cornell is forging ahead, now it is a half length, a length, that Cornell leads, she crosses the line, the race is won! There comes a tremendous burst of cheering that is accompanied by the ringing of bells, with long blasts from the whistles of the excursion steamers and is punctuated by metallic toots from the countless motor boats" (1917, pp. 251–52).

sity's Ithaca environs. The 1873 *Cornellian* year-book noted that "the Cornell Navy" and a Tom Hughes Club had been formed in 1871. The 1874 *Cornellian* listed both Tom Hughes and Goldwin Smith among the club's honorary members. The club's active membership that year listed eight officers and 98 student names. The 1874 yearbook also noted that the Class of '76 boat club had won the Tom Hughes Cup that year.

It didn't hurt, either, that two educational institutions which Cornell faculty and students perhaps sought to emulate—Yale and Harvard (though Hughes spoke disparagingly of Harvard's chapel, library, clubs, educational system, and games)—made rowing a major sport.

The Cornell Navy's first rowing coach also was a student and a team rower. John Nelson Ostrom of East Randolph, the "father of Cornell rowing," entered Cornell in the early 1870s and received his B.C.E. in 1877 and C.E. in 1895. Coach Ostrom was followed by notable and legendary coaches such as Charles E. Courtney (coach from 1888–1920) and R. Harrison "Stork" Sanford (coach from 1937–70).

It didn't take Cornell long to achieve fame among rowers. In 1873, Cornell's first crew of eight competed. In 1874, the class of 1877 rowers won first prize and the Watkins Regatta Trophy, which is still used today to christen new boats with Cayuga Lake finish-line water. The next year, Cornell scored a double victory in a three-mile event at the Saratoga Race. The freshman team defeated Harvard by five seconds, as well as Brown and Princeton behind Harvard, with a time of 17:32:15. The varsity six-oared team, under the cadence set by stroke John Ostrom, beat second-place Columbia by 11 seconds,

with a time of 16:53:15. Eleven other teams finished behind Cornell and Columbia. *The Cornellian* of 1875–76 reported that "Ithaca [was] in a state of eruption over the double victory." Cornell rowers established a world's record in the three-mile race, with a time of 14:27:30 on June 25, 1891, at New London, Connecticut, defeating Penn and Columbia. The team of 1957, the best Cornell rowers

ever—"undefeated, untied, and world's champion—was written up in a two-page *Sports Illustrated* spread on July 15, when it beat arch-rival Yale by half a length with a time of 6:53 to win the Henley Royal Regatta in England.

Cornell was a charter member of the Intercollegiate Rowing Association, along with Pennsylvania and Columbia. The IRA is the premier sanctioning

on a trestle are glimpsed in the left background). Cornell towers are shadows on the left distant horizon. Undergraduates stand in the doorways, the one on the right proudly wearing his Cornell letter sweater. A large front-wheeled bicycle with a mustache handlebar leans against the southern wall of the building. To the right of the building stands a buggy and driver, the horse covered with a blanket.

The present boathouse (given in 1957 by John L. Collyer '17, president of B. F. Goodrich for many years, as well as long-time chair of the Cornell board of trustees), stands on virtually the same location. Two eight-man crews are seen in their boats on the water. Female rowers prepare their launch from left dockside. Women rowed in the

body of the sport. A silver Varsity Challenge Cup was presented to the IRA in 1898 by Dr. Louis L. Seaman of Cornell and goes to the winner of the Men's Heavyweight Varsity national championship. Not surprisingly, Cornell leads all schools in the number of times the University has won the Varsity Challenge Cup (26 in the 105-year history of the IRA, with second-place Navy winning 12 times).

Shown in the historic photograph (opposite) by McGillivray is the varsity eight-oared crew and coxswain in front of the University Boathouse on the east bank of the Cayuga Inlet, which replaced an earlier building on the north bank of Cascadilla Creek near the Inlet. This building, gift of the graduating class of 1890, was near the Lackawanna railroad station (Delaware, Lackawanna, and Western boxcars

early twentieth century before women's crew became an official Cornell varsity sport in 1975 as a result of Title IX. Some 150 students (including 50 women) and more than 60 water craft (2-oar, 4-oar, and 8-oar) are associated with Cornell rowing. Freshman and varsity teams, both lightweight and heavyweight, compete in each category. Races are 2,000 meters, the Olympic distance.

EPILOGUE
Spaces in Transition

The open spaces remaining on or near the main campus are tempting sites for building expansion. None are quite as delicious morsels as the athletic-related asphalts and greens. If nature abhors a vacuum, so too does a modern, ambitious university abhor open space, it would seem.

In 1903 the trustees designated 57 acres of the former university farm for a "playground" and athletic field. A period of conflict emerged, pitting the land needs of the College of Agriculture against the field needs of athletics. Athletics won the right to "Alumni Field," named to honor the many alumni who cumulatively gave several hundred thousands of dollars toward grading, drainage, planting, and equipping the field, which opened with a May 1915 track meet. The area has been used, torn up for buried construction projects, and resodded for decades. Notably, the Cornell Electron Storage Ring, a high-luminosity electron-positron collider used by nearby Wilson Synchrotron Laboratory (built in 1965–66) to create new matter, runs in a tunnel 15 meters beneath the surface.

Some inroads on claiming the area have been made by the College of Agriculture and Life Sciences. The western lower area, where football games once were played, has been whittled away by the construction of Dale R. Corson–Seeley G. Mudd Halls, Comstock Hall, and the Biotechnology Building.

Pictured in the foreground are the tennis courts east of Bartels Hall (also known as "The Field House," left, middle), the remnants of Alumni Field (now known as Robison Alumni Fields and the Robert J. Kane Sports Complex), and Bradfield Hall on the horizon. The precious grass athletic field, used by men's and women's varsity soccer, women's lacrosse, and by the football and sprint football teams, stretches between Tower Road on the north, Stocking (1923), Wing (1913), and Riley-Robb (1956) Halls on the east, Campus Road and related buildings (Bartels Hall and Lynah Skating Rink) on the south, and the Biotechnology Building on the west.

The new buildings that will occupy the space are a \$110 million Life Sciences Technology building, which will consume 240,000 square feet or nearly half the existing fields, and a wrestling facility. The Life Sciences Technology building will be designed by Richard Meyers, a Cornell alum and well-known architect. Construction will begin in late 2003. Scholars from many disciplines will focus on studies "of the revolution that's taking place in the biological sciences," according to Henrik N. Dullea '61, Vice President of University Relations, cited in the *Ithaca Journal*.

Before the board of trustees rendered its decision on the fate of the site in late January 2002, the Life Sciences Technology building had renewed the debate of nearly a century before; this time, forces aligned with the College of Agriculture and Life Sciences have had the last word in the battle with athletics over use of the space. New replacement fields for men's and women's varsity soccer teams, the women's lacrosse team, and the varsity and sprint football teams will be located a considerable distance away. Meanwhile, a different sport claims the area occupied by the tennis courts in the photograph. The \$3 million Friedman Wrestling Center for Cornell's 40-plus wrestlers (two of whom won All-American honors in the spring of 2002) and 1,000 spectators began service fall semester 2002. The wrestling squad has won the Ivy League title three times since 1993. Over its history, the Big Red wrestling program has won the Ivies 23 times.

PHILLIPS HALL, KNIGHT LABORATORY, UPSON, GRUMMAN, & RHODES HALLS

Buildings pictured are, from left to right: Phillips Hall, Knight Laboratory (white, foreground), Grumman Hall (white, background), Rhodes Hall (background) and Upson Hall. They will be in the shadow of Duffield Hall, a $58.5 million high-tech research center that, once constructed, will be one of the world's most sophisticated nanotechnology centers. The Duffield Nanofabrication Facility and Nano-biotechnology Center is being built on the engineering quad, south of the intersection of Campus Road and East Avenue. It is scheduled for completion in May 2004. The new center will boast the very latest in electronic, photonic, biotechnology, and micro-electromechanical devices, along with advanced materials processing capabilities. Nanotechnology, the manipulation of materials on atomic or molecular levels to build microscopic devices, such as robots, is a longtime Cornell focus. The Cornell Nanofabrication Facility is the country's oldest federally sponsored nanotechnology center. The construction project will tie Duffield Hall with Phillips and Upson Halls through an atrium that

promises to be winter-friendly and a relaxed space for faculty and student interaction. The old Knight lab will be demolished at the end of 2003, and a new Knight Lab will be incorporated into Duffield.

While the loss of the trees in the foreground is regrettable, the denuding of the engineering grounds for construction purposes is salved by knowledge that an internationally famous landscape architectural firm

has been engaged to oversee regrading of the engineering quad. The firm's design will provide advanced lighting, seating, and pathways, as well as make new plantings once the new center is completed.

KENNEDY HALL, PLANT SCIENCE BUILDING, & BRADFIELD HALL

East across the patio from the archway between Kennedy and Roberts Halls, an empty space where the old Roberts Hall once stood tempts those who plan new buildings. The footprint is small, however, so a building constructed there probably will be both deep and tall, joining Bradfield Hall, visible in the distance beyond the Plant Science Building, in agricultural-quad skyscraper status.

RAND HALL

Unrelated construction in the foreground offers a glimpse of what is to come for Rand Hall. Erected in 1912 at the corner of University and East Avenues, Rand Hall has contained machine and pattern shops and an electrical laboratory. The building is a memorial to Jasper Raymond Rand and Addison Crittenden Rand, founders of the Rand Drill Company (later merged into the Ingersoll-Rand Company), and to Jasper Raymond Rand, Jr., class of 1897. In its last gasp, the old building has housed the College of Architecture, Art, and Planning undergraduate architecture program, with studio space, faculty offices, computer labs, classrooms, and shops.

A $10 million gift from Irma Milstein and family in honor of husband and father Paul Milstein, prominent New York City developer of residential and commercial real estate properties, will help create Milstein Hall to provide modern architecture program facilities for the top-ranked program in the nation. The architect will be the Berlin firm Barkow Leibinger. Frank Barkow, one of the firm's founders, was a visiting art critic at Cornell 1990–92. Construction is expected to begin in fall 2004. There is no word yet on whether the traditional dragon, annually constructed in Rand Hall for spring Dragon Day by generations of freshmen architecture students, approves of plans for its new digs.

NOYES LODGE

Cornell University offers instruction in more than thirty languages. Noyes Lodge serves as a Language Resource Center. It makes available a wide variety of services for students and teachers in Chinese, Dutch, French, German, Hebrew, Hindi, Intensive English, Italian, Sinhala, and Spanish. Facilities include a language media center with audio and video tapes for playback, a video classroom, a Macintosh-equipped classroom (12 double carrels, four single carrels, plus a teacher station, each with computers with basic web and word processing software and Internet connection), and a seminar room. Services offered include workshops, speeches, bibliographies, and assistance with materials development (audio, video). It occupies a key location near the Alumni House on the north side of Fall Creek, between the Triphammer Footbridge and the Thurston Avenue Bridge. This has led to plans that note its potential as an excellent site for a future visitor center.

NOYES COMMUNITY CENTER & U-HALLS

On West Campus, temporary buildings were replaced by the 1952–54 residence buildings nicknamed "U-Halls," (University Class Halls of '17, '18, '22, '26, and '28). Together with Sperry Hall, they are plotted in a cluster with Noyes Community Center at the westernmost edge, east of Stewart Avenue. They are scheduled for demolition. Persons with acute architectural appreciation probably won't miss them. The U-Halls have been described as "brick boxes standing on bare plots of ground" (Parsons, 1968, p. 262). They were constructed during an era in which Cornell had finally emerged from debt to solvency. The trustees were in no mind to fritter away the financial reserves with frilly Gothic structures such as the West Campus residences farther up the hill, contributed during World War I and the postwar era by individuals such as George F. Baker and George C. Boldt.

The new $200 million-plus West Campus will be completed in phases, with the first building opening fall 2004 and the remaining four in place by 2010. The living-learning residential houses will provide space for about

350 students each, mostly sophomores, but also transfer students, juniors, and seniors. Each house will have its own green, dining room, common room, library, music practice room, mailroom, and guest suite. There also will be a West Campus Community Recreation Center for

all 1,800 residents. The new West Campus complex will promote interaction among students, the half-dozen resident graduate and professional tutors, and "house professor" in each residence, while retaining links with academic programs. The hope is to build residences that will lend them-

selves to a creative and natural sense of community and intellectual engagement, continuing a process that the North Campus initiative sought for freshmen. The intention also is to further strengthen students' leadership and governance interests and initiatives. This dream builds on the exist-

"The West Campus initiative is based on a 'house system' that emphasizes informal interaction with faculty members, opportunities for personal and intellectual growth, self-governance, social and cultural programming, privacy and independence. A Cornell faculty member will reside in each house as a house professor or dean. A staff person will serve as assistant dean, and graduate students will act as mentors. An elected house council, chaired by the house professor and composed primarily of resident students, will govern the house and develop social, intellectual, athletic and cultural programs and activities."

—President Hunter R. Rawlings III, *State of the University Address*, 2001

ing Faculty-in-Residence program by offering enhanced living quarters for faculty, graduate students, and staff. Additionally, it seeks to advance the traditional Faculty Fellow and the A. D. White Professors-at-Large programs by offering communal dining, seminar space, and offices to some thirty faculty members per residence, who will not live in the houses as their primary or permanent residence, but who will be encouraged to spend considerable time and energy there. Plans call for advanced access to computer-based services and further enhancing the West Campus living experience through additional cultural, entertainment, and physical fitness facilities and opportunities, thus promoting the experience of West Campus as a personalized neighborhood.

"Too many people try to evaluate a university education on the basis of what you can do with it; more often the true measure of its importance lies in what it does to you."
— *Romeyn Berry*

BIBLIOGRAPHY

Abt, Henry Edward (1926). *Ithaca: Its Origin and Growth*. Ithaca: Ross W. Kellogg.

Altschuler, Glen C. (1979). *Andrew D. White—Educator, Historian, Diplomat*. Ithaca: Cornell University Press.

Becker, Carl L. (1943). *Cornell University: Founders and the Founding*. Ithaca: Cornell University Press.

Bellamy, Laurie E. (1983, October). "The First Women at Cornell," *Cornell Countryman*, pp. 4–5.

Berry, Romeyn (1927). *Sport Stuff by RB*. Ithaca: The Cayuga Press.

Berry, Romeyn (1950). *Behind the Ivy: Fifty Years in One University with Visits to Sundry Others*. Ithaca: Cornell University Press.

Berry, Skip (1990). *Gordon Parks*. New York: Chelsea House Publishers.

Bishop, Morris (1962). *A History of Cornell*. Ithaca: Cornell University Press.

Bitz, Bob (2001, Winter). "Cornell Was Advocate for Agricultural Innovations," *The Cultivator*, New York State Agricultural Society, p. 6.

Block, Robin C. (1983, October). "Spring Day! Full of Amusement," *Cornell Countryman*, pp. 6–7.

Borthwick, Pamela C. (1983, October). "LLENROC, Ezra's House Turned Fraternity," *Cornell Countryman*, p. 18.

Bourke-White, Margaret (1963). *Portrait of Myself*. New York: Simon and Schuster.

Brann, Ross, Edna R. Dugan., Eugene

C. Erickson, John L. Ford, Donald H. King, Isaac Kramnick, Michelle A. Schaffer, and Karen M. Taxier (1998, September 23). "Transforming West Campus." [http://ri.campuslife. cornell.edu/west.html].

Branscomb, Jon, Fred Ciesla, Sam LaRoque, and Eldar Noe (1998). "Team 318's Pumpkin Project." Ithaca: Cornell University. [http://www.news.cornell.edu/releases /March98/pumpkin/318.html].

Brown, Theodore M. (1972). *Margaret Bourke-White: Photojournalist*. Ithaca: Cornell University.

Bryant, Edward (1977). *Clara Seley, Jason Seley, Sculpture*. Syracuse: Everson Museum of Art, Exhibit, January 22–February 27.

Callahan, Sean (1972). *The Photographs of Margaret Bourke-White*. New York: New York Graphic Society.

Campi, Esther (2001, October 20). "World Events Place Focus on Core Values at CU." *Ithaca Journal*, pp. 1A, 9A.

Campi, Esther (2001, October 20). "CU: Campus Remains Too White." *Ithaca Journal*, p. 1B.

Campi, Esther (2002, March 16). "Rawlings Chalks It Up: Cornell President Prefers a Return to Teaching," *Ithaca Journal*, pp. 1A–3A.

Campi, Esther (2002, March 27). "CU Gathers Student Input on West Campus," *Ithaca Journal*, pp. 1B, 3B.

Campus Unrest at Cornell (1969,

September 5). Ithaca: Report of the Special Trustee Committee, The Office of University Publications.

Carron, Malcolm (1956). *The Contract Colleges of Cornell University: A Co-operative Educational Enterprise*. Ithaca: Cornell University Press.

Case, Harry L., ed. (1930). *A Half-Century at Cornell 1880–1930*. Ithaca: *The Cornell Daily Sun*, Inc.

Cofer, Rebecca H. (1990). *The Straight Story: An Informal History of Willard Straight Hall 1925–90*. Ithaca: Cornell University.

"College Names New Officers: Nomination of Jason Seley as Dean," (1980, Spring). *College of Architecture, Art, and Planning Alumni Newsletter*, p. 2.

Colman, Gould P. (1963). *Education & Agriculture: A History of the New York State College of Agriculture at Cornell University*. Ithaca: Cornell University.

Conable, Charlotte Williams (1977). *Women at Cornell: The Myth of Equal Education*. Ithaca: Cornell University Press.

Cornell, Alonzo B. (1884). *"True and Firm." Biography of Ezra Cornell, Founder of the Cornell University. A Filial Tribute*. New York: A. S. Barnes & Company.

Cornell Collection of Regional History: Fifth and Sixth Annual Reports of the Curator 1948–1950. Ithaca: Cornell University.

Cornell Department of Architecture (2001, January 31). "Top 15 Schools

and Colleges of Architecture. 1. Cornell University." [http://www.architecture.cornell.edu/ newsevents/pressreleases/ CornellArchNews.html].

Cornell School of Hotel Administration (2001). [http://www.hotelschool. cornell.edu/].

Cornell Law School (2001). [http://www.lawschool.cornell.edu/].

Cornellian, The (1871–1872). Ithaca: Secret Societies.

Cornellian, The (1873). Ithaca: Secret Societies.

Cornellian, The (1874). Ithaca: Secret Societies.

Cornellian, The (1905). Springfield, Mass.: The F. A. Bassette Company.

Charles William Curtis and Stephanie Marx Curtis Papers, 1884–1916. Division of Rare and Manuscript Collections 14-21-547, Carl A. Kroch Library, Cornell University.

Damon, Mackenzie (2002, March 26). "West Campus Suites Showcased," *Cornell Daily Sun*, pp. 1, 8.

Davis, John Yawger (1868). "Letter from a Cornell Student, October 1868," pp. 170–172 in Carl L. Becker (1943). *Cornell University: Founders and the Founding*. Ithaca: Cornell University Press.

Davis, Katherine (2000, October 2). "$10 Million Given to Replace Rand Hall," *Cornell Daily Sun* [http:// www.cornelldailysun.com/articles/ 509/].

Bibliography

150

Day, Edmund Ezra (1952). "Of Loyalties," pp. 187–190 in Milton R. Konvitz, ed., *Education for Freedom and Responsibility: Selected Essays by Edmund Ezra Day*. Ithaca: Cornell University Press.

Dennis, James M. (1967). *Karl Bitter: Architectural Sculptor 1867–1915*. Madison: The University of Wisconsin Press.

Dethlefsen, Edgar Raymond (1957). *William Henry Miller Papers, 1890–1957*. Division of Rare and Manuscript Collections 1856, Carl A. Kroch Library, Cornell University.

Dieckmann, Jane Marsh (1986). *A Short History of Tompkins County*. Ithaca: Dewitt Historical Society of Tompkins County.

Dimunation, Mark G., and Elaine D. Engst (1996). *A Legacy of Ideas: Andrew Dickson White and the Founding of the Cornell University Library*. Ithaca: Cornell University Library.

Dorf, Philip (1965). *The Builder: A Biography of Ezra Cornell*. Ithaca: Pine Grove Press.

Eddy, Christen (2001, April 19). "Architects Share Their Milstein Hall Designs." *Cornell Daily Sun*. [http://www.cornelldailysun.com/articles/2646].

Edmondson, Brad (1996). *Hospitality Leadership: The Cornell Hotel School*. Ithaca: Cornell Society of Hotelmen.

Frank, Maggie (2002, March 25). "Rawlings to Step Down: President Will Retire in 2003," *Cornell Daily Sun*, pp. 1, 14.

Friedland, William H., and Harry Edwards (1973). "Confrontation at Cornell," pp. 83–103 in Howard S. Becker, ed., *Campus Power Struggle*, second edition. New Brunswick, N.J.: Transaction Books.

Friedlander, Blaine P., Jr. (1998, April 2). "Cornell Releases Kingsbury Commission Finding: 'It Is a Pumpkin!'" Cornell News Service. [http://www.news.cornell.edu/releases/April98/PumpkinDecision.bpf.html].

Furman, John R. (1986). "Crew: A History That Endures," *Wearers of the C*. Ithaca: Cayuga Press, pp. 32–33.

Gaffney, Patricia H., ed. (1974). *The Willard Straight Papers at Cornell University 1857–1925*. Ithaca: Department of Manuscripts and University Archives, John M. Olin Library.

Geddes, Darryl (1997, April 1). "Olive Tjaden, pioneering architect who designed more than 400 Garden City, L. I., homes, dies at 92." Cornell News Service. [http://www.news.cornell.edu/releases/April97/tjadenobit.dg.html].

Geddes, Darryl (1997, September 11). "Tjaden Hall steeple is rebuilt as part of major renovation project. Crane will lift 20-ton steeple into place week of Sept. 22." Cornell News Service. [http://www.news.cornell.edu/releases/Sept97/steeple_advisory.dg.html].

Geddes, Darryl (1997, October 2). "Olive Tjaden Hall steeple returns to Arts Quad." *Cornell Chronicle*. [http://www.news.cornell.edu//Chronicle/97/10.2.97/Tjaden.html].

Geddes, Darryl (1998, January 22). "Olive Tjaden Hall reopens after complete renovation of interior." *Cornell Chronicle*. [http://www.news.cornell.edu//Chronicle/98/1.22.98/Tjaden.html].

Gerbracht, Steve (1998, March 13). *A Tale of Two Pumpkins*. Cornell University. [http://www.news.cornell.edu/releases/March98/pumpkin/Tale_of_Two.html].

Gold, Martha (2002, September 25). "W. Campus Neighbors Speak Out." The Ithaca Journal [http://theithaca-journal.com].

Goulden, Joseph C. (1976). *The Best Years: 1945–1950*. New York: Atheneum.

Guerlac, Rita (1962). *An Introduction to Cornell*. New York: Cornell University.

Guide to the Campus of Cornell University (1920). Ithaca: Cornell University.

Guess, Andrew (2002, September 25). "Disagreement Continues Over AA&P. Future of Cornell's Smallest College Still in the Air." *Cornell Daily Sun* [http://www.cornelldailysun.com/articles/6104/].

Guess, Andrew (2002, November 11). "Barkow Leibinger Replace Holl as Milstein Architects: Committee Chooses Lesser Known Firm to Design Architecture College's New Home" *Cornell Daily Sun* [http://www.cornelldailysun.com/articles/6843/].

Hankin, Stephanie (2002, January 28). "Trustees Approve New Building Site: Alumni Fields," *Cornell Daily Sun*, pp. 1, 8.

Hankin, Stephanie (2002, August 8). "Cornell and Milstein Hall Architect Parts Ways." *Cornell Daily Sun* [http://www.cornelldailysun.com/articles/5734/].

Hart, James Morgan (1913, March 25). *Ezra Cornell: The First Goldwin Smith Lecture Delivered on Founder's Day, January 11th*. Ithaca: Cornell University.

Haultain, Arnold, ed. (1910). *Goldwin Smith Reminiscences*. New York: Macmillan.

Heller, Lillian (1954). *Boarding House Student Scrapbook, 1944–1954*. Division of Rare and Manuscript Collections, 37-5-2857, Carl A. Kroch Library, Cornell University.

Herskovits, Beth (2001, November 15). "Victory Club Parties with Good Cause," *The Cornell Daily Sun*, pp. 7, 11.

Hewitt, Waterman Thomas (1905). *Cornell University: A History* (4 vols.). New York: The University Publishing Society.

Hickerson, H. Thomas, and Elaine D. Engst (1990, Fall). "A Truly American University," *Documentation Newsletter* XVI:2. Ithaca: Department of Manuscripts and University Archives,

Cornell University Libraries.

Higgins, Dan (2002, December 16). "Cornell Taps Grad as President. Michigan Law Dean Lehman to Take Post in July 2003." *Ithaca Journal,* p.1A.

Hill, David (2001, March 27). "Campus Trucks Serve Up Tradition," *Ithaca Journal,* p. 2A.

Inauguration of Cornell University, The (1921). Reprinted from the Account of the Proceedings at the Inauguration October 7th, 1868. Ithaca: Cornell University.

International Students & Scholars Office of the Mario Einaudi Center for International Studies (2001). *2000–2001 Statistical Report.* Ithaca: Cornell University.

Jacklin, Kathleen, ed. (1974). *Cornell University Collection of Regional History and the University Archives Report of the Curator and Archivist, 1962–1966.* Ithaca: Cornell University Libraries.

Johnson Graduate School of Management (2001, August 29). "Ph.D. Program Areas of Study" [http://www.johnson.cornell.edu/ admissions/phd/].

Jones, Scott (2002, March 26). "Cornell Claims Two Wrestling All-Americans," *Cornell Daily Sun* [http://cornelldaily-sun.com/articles/5074/].

Kammen, Carol (2001, September 15). "Cornell's Forgotten Father Deserves Credit," *Ithaca Journal,* p. 1B.

Kane, Robert J. (1992). *Good Sports: A History of Cornell Athletics.* Ithaca: Cornell University.

Kingsbury, John M., Molly Kyle Jahn, Henry Munger, Dominick Paolillo, and Anusuya Rangarajan (1998, March 24). *Report of the Expert Panel Examining the Unidentified Object Removed (By Force) from the Distal Portion of McGraw Bell Tower on Friday, March 13, 1998.* Cornell University [http://www.news.cornell.edu/releases /March98/pumpkin/Panel.html].

Kountoupes, Nicola (1998, June 25). "New light in Sage Hall." *Cornell Chronicle* [http://www.news. cornell.edu//Chronicle/98/6.25.98/ photo-Sage_atrium.html].

Kramnick, Isaac (2002, Summer). "Q & A: A Tale of Two Campuses," *Communique,* Cornell University Division of Alumni Affairs and Development, pp. 6–7, 18.

Kreig, Andrew (1969). "The End of a Bizarre Era," pp. 6–7 in David Margulis, ed. (1980). *A Century at Cornell.* Ithaca: The Cornell Daily Sun, Inc.

Language Resource Center at Cornell University (2001). [http://dml. cornell.edu].

Laws and Documents Relating to Cornell University 1862–1883 (1883). Ithaca.

Lee, Donald (2001, April 19). "All You Wanted to Know About Crew." *Cornell Daily Sun.* [http://www.cornell dailysun.com/articles/2643/].

Lent, B. F. (1900). *Songs of Cornell.* Ithaca: Lent Publishing.

Litvak, Annie (1999, November 11). "Homecoming fanfare culminates events rededicating chimes." *Cornell Chronicle.* [http://www.news. cornell.edu//Chronicle/99/11.11.99 /chimes_rededication.html].

Lowery, George (2001, Summer). "Crew: Pulling Ahead," *Communique,* Cornell University Division of Alumni Affairs and Development, p. 14.

Lowery, George (2002, Summer). "A Community Design: Cornell's Investment in Undergraduate Education," *Communique,* Cornell University Division of Alumni Affairs and Development, pp. 8–9.

Maas, James B., Megan L. Wherry, David J. Alexrod, Barbara R. Hogan, and Jennifer A. Blumin (1998). *Power Sleep.* New York: Villard.

Mack, Edward C., and W. H. G. Armytage (1952). *Thomas Hughes: The Life of the Author of Tom Brown's Schooldays.* London: Ernest Benn Limited.

Margulis, Daniel, ed. (1980). *A Century at Cornell.* Ithaca: *The Cornell Daily Sun,* Inc.

Military Records of Cornell University in the World War (1930). Ithaca: Cornell University.

McKeown, Ed (1991). *The Cornell Chimes: In Celebration of the Hundredth Anniversary of McGraw Tower.* Ithaca: Cornell University.

Mica, Jim (1997 November 26). "The Great Cornell Pumpkin." [http://www.home.tiac.net/cri/1997/ pumpkin/html].

Miller, Ellen (2002, February 6). "Architect Introduces Plan for West Campus," *Cornell Daily Sun,* pp. 1, 11.

Mosley, Kandea (2002, January 28). "CU OKs Sciences Facility Site," *Ithaca Journal,* pp. 1A, 4A.

Norlander, Peter (2002, March 25). "Rawlings to Step Down: Tenure Leaves Mark," *Cornell Daily Sun,* pp. 1, 13.

"Olive Tjaden VanSickle–Distinguished Alumna," (1980, Spring). *College of Architecture, Art, and Planning Alumni Newsletter,* p. 1.

O'Neill, William L. (1971). *Coming Apart: An Informal History of America in the 1960s.* New York: Quadrangle Books.

Parks, Gordon (1997). *Half Past Autumn: A Retrospective.* Boston: Bulfinch Press.

Parsons, Kermit Carlyle (1968). *The Cornell Campus: A History of Its Planning and Development.* Ithaca: Cornell University Press.

Poole, Murray Edward (1916). *A Story Historical of Cornell University with Biographies of Distinguished Cornellians.* Ithaca: The Cayuga Press.

Pope, Alexander (trans.) (1891). *The Odyssey of Homer.* London: W. W. Gibbings.

Proceedings and Addresses at the Laying of the Corner Stone of the Cornell University Laboratory of Chemistry. (1921, October 20). Ithaca: Cornell University.

Qiu, Weining (1998). *Pumpkin Contest.* Ithaca: Cornell University. [http://www.news.cornell.edu/releases/March98/pumpkin/qiu.html].

Rawlings, Hunter R. III (2001, October 19). "State of the University Address." [http://www.news.cornell.edu/campus/stateofuniv0110.html].

"Rawlings Announces His Intention to Step Down in 2003" (2002, March 21). *Cornell Chronicle*, pp. 1, 4.

Rhodes, Frank H. T. (1997). *Successful Fund Raising for Higher Education: The Advancement of Learning* (Phoenix: The Oryx Press).

Rhodes, Frank H. T. (2001). *The Creation of the Future: The Role of the American University.* Ithaca: Cornell University Press.

Roberts, Isaac Phillips (1946). *Autobiography of a Farm Boy.* Ithaca: Cornell University Press.

Sage Chapel. (Undated). No. 372 10M A. Ithaca, NY: Cornell University.

Samuels, Kelly (2001, March 12). Dragon Day Rivalry Neared. *Cornell Daily Sun.* [http://www.cornelldailysun.com/articles/2129/].

Sanderson. James Gardner (1898). *Cornell Stories.* New York: Charles Scribner's Sons.

Sandler, Martin W. (1989). *American*

Image: Photographing One Hundred Fifty Years in the Life of a Nation. Chicago: Contemporary Books, Inc.

Schafer, Allegra (1998, March). "The Truth About Me, the McGraw Tower Pumpkin." [http://www.news.cornell.edu/releases/March98/pumpkin/Truth.html].

Schroeder, Heather (2001, November 8). "Life Sciences Building Site Still Up in the Air," *The Cornell Daily Sun*, pp. 1, 8.

Schroeder, Heather (2001, December 7). "Trustee Committee Approves Plans for West Campus," *The Cornell Daily Sun*, pp. 1, 8.

Sheldon, Seth L. (1897). *Photographic Gems, Being a Collection of Views of Cornell University.* Ithaca: Press of Andrus and Church.

Sisler, Carol U. (2001, January 27). "Walking Tour Reveals Architect Miller's Influence," *Ithaca Journal*, p. 2A.

Sisler, Carol U. (2001, November 3). "Collegetown Has Ever-changing Past," *The Ithaca Journal*, p. 1B.

Slon, Michael (1998). *Songs From the Hill: A History of the Cornell University Glee Club.* Ithaca: Cornell University Glee Club.

Smith, Albert W. (1934). *Ezra Cornell: A Character Study.* Ithaca: William A. Church Company.

Smith, Goldwin (1904). *The Early Days of Cornell.* Ithaca: Andrus and Church, Printers.

Sokol, Thomas A. (1988). *Songs of Cornell.* Ithaca: Cornell University Glee Club.

Strout, Cushing, and David I. Grossvogel, eds. (1970). *Divided We Stand: Reflections on the Crisis at Cornell.* Garden City, N.Y.: Doubleday & Company.

Swieringa, Robert J. "Our Direction" [http://www.johnson.cornell.edu/dean/].

The Class of 1871 (1930). *The First Three Classes at Cornell University.* Ithaca: The Cayuga Press.

Thomas, Alison (2001, October 17). "Alumni Fields May Be Site of Future Genomics Building," *The Cornell Daily Sun*, pp. 1, 8.

Thomas, M. Carey (1897). "Mr. Sage and Co-Education," pp. 51–62 in *Memorial Exercises in Honor of Henry Williams Sage.* Ithaca: Cornell University.

Trousdale, J. B. (1967). *Cornell University First Century–Lands & Buildings 1867–1967.* Ithaca: Controller's Office.

Valentine, Jeff, for The Materials Research Society's Pumpkin Team (1998). *Pumpkin or PumpCON? An Analysis of Unknown Compounds at High Altitude.* Ithaca: Cornell University [http://www.news.cornell.edu/releases/March98/pumpkin/PumpCON.html].

Various authors (1939). *Our Cornell.* Ithaca: Cornell Alumni Association.

Van Sickle, Kenny (1986). "Remember-

ing the Days of Stork Sanford," *Wearers of the C.* Ithaca: Cayuga Press, pp. 34-35.

von Engeln, O. D. (1909). *At Cornell.* Ithaca: The Artil Co. Publishers.

von Engeln, O. D. (1917). *Concerning Cornell.* Ithaca: Geography Supply Bureau Publishers.

Ward, William B. (2000). *History of the Department of Communication at Cornell University.* Ithaca: Cornell University Print Shop.

Wasserman, Aliza (2002, March 26). "Rhodes Recovering, in Good Spirits," *Cornell Daily Sun*, p. 7.

Welch, Paula D. (1999). *Silver Era, Golden Moments: A Celebration of Ivy League Women's Athletics.* Lanham, Md.: Madison Books.

West, John R. (1994). *Memories of Golden Sports Years at Cornell University 1953–1989.* Lansing, N.Y.: Weidenhammer Printers.

White, Andrew D. (1905). *Autobiography of Andrew Dickson White with Portraits* (Vols. 1–2). New York: The Century Co.

White, Horatio Stevens (1925). *Willard Fiske, Life and Correspondence; a Biographical Study, by His Literary Executor.* New York: Oxford University Press.

Willey, Sarah (2001, September 7). "No Temporary Site Yet Named for AA&P." *Cornell Daily Sun* [http://www.cornelldailysun.com/articles/2977/].

Williams, Ronald John (1949). *Jennie McGraw Fiske: Her Influence Upon Cornell University*. Ithaca: Cornell University Press.

Wilson Synchrotron Laboratory. [http://www.lns.cornell.edu/public/lab-info/wilson.html].

Young, Charles V. P. (1954). *Cornell In Pictures: 1868–1954*. Ithaca: Cornell University Press.

Young, Charles V. P., and H. A. Stevenson, (1965). *Cornell in Pictures: The First Century*. Ithaca, N.Y.: Quill and Dagger Alumni Association.

"$2M Trust Aids Cornell's Renovation of White Hall" (2002, May 9). *Ithaca Journal*, p. 1B.

Maps

Prentiss, A. N. (1871, November 1). *Map of the Cornell University Estate*.

Burleigh, Lucien R., and J. Lyth (1882). *Ithaca, N. Y.* American Memory Map Collections 1544–1999. [http://memory.loc.gov/cgi-bin/map_item.pl].

Cornell University Campus (1891). In Kermit Carlyle Parsons (1968), p. 123. *The Cornell Campus: A History of Its Planning and Development*. Ithaca: Cornell University Press.

Cornell University Campus (1900). In Gould P. Colman (1963), p. 337. *Education & Agriculture: A History of the New York State College of Agriculture at Cornell University*. Ithaca: Cornell University.

Cornell University Campus (1903, July 15). In Kermit Carlyle Parsons (1968), p. 189. *The Cornell Campus: A History of Its Planning and Development*. Ithaca: Cornell University Press.

Cornell University Campus (1905). The Campus of Cornell University, Ithaca, N.Y. (1951).

Cornell University (2001, August). Ithaca, N.Y.: Facilities Planning.

Map of Ithaca (1942). H. A. Manning Company. Schenectady, N.Y.

PHOTO CREDITS

INDEX

Italicized page numbers refer to photographs

THE AUTHORS

Harry Littell grew up in Alfred, New York. His work focuses on the communities, architecture, and landscape of the upstate region. Since moving to Ithaca in 1991, he has worked as a carpenter, artist, and photographer. In the fall of 2000, McBooks Press of Ithaca published Littell's revised and updated version of *Ithaca Then & Now* by Merrill Hesch and Richard Pieper, which compares historical and contemporary views of the city's built environment. Littell holds an A.A.S. in photography from the Rochester Institute of Technology, a B.F.A. in fine arts from Cornell University, and an M.F.A. in sculpture from the New York State College of Ceramics at Alfred University. His sculptures and photographs have been shown at galleries and museums including the Sheldon Memorial Art Gallery in Lincoln, Nebraska; the Memorial Art Gallery in Rochester, New York; The Everson Museum of Art in Syracuse, New York; the Arnot Museum in Elmira, New York; the State of the Art Gallery in Ithaca, New York; and the Tompkins County Museum in Ithaca, New York. He lives with his wife, Patricia Fox, and two daughters, Nora and Charlotte.

Ronald E. Ostman grew up in International Falls, Minnesota. His social science work has focused on the content of mass media of communication, the effects of mediated messages on individuals and groups, and processes of public opinion and persuasion. He is the author of several academic books and many scholarly journal articles. His other book dealing with photography was published with Jack Delano, former Farm Security Administration/Office of War Information photographer, and fellow academic Professor Royal D. Colle. It is titled *Superfortress Over Japan: 24 Hours with a B-29* (Motorbooks International Publishers, 1996). Ostman holds a Ph.D. and M.A. in journalism and mass communication from the University of Minnesota and a B.A. in English from Bemidji State University. He is professor and chair of the Department of Communication at Cornell University, where he has taught and conducted research since 1979. Ostman lives near Lansing with his wife, Nancy Ostman, Natural Areas Director of Cornell Plantations. Their children are RaeEllen, of El Sobrante, California, and Andrew, of New York City. Five Cornell degrees are held by the members of his family—one Ph.D., one M.Eng., and three bachelor degrees.